International Praise for
Mud Pies to Blue Skies

"The king of storytelling keeps you entertained and engaged. Randy Ray opens up about his poverty-stricken childhood telling stories he's never told before. A genuine must-read."
— Flora Li, Triple Diamond Director, USA

"Thank you, Randy, for writing such an open and illuminating memoir. Your honesty and zest for life shines through, and your commitment to helping others is an inspiration to all."
— Stefania Lo Gatto, Double Diamond Director, Italy

"The colorful stories overflow with Randy's humor, faith, and fighting spirit. *Mud Pies to Blue Skies* is a passport for anyone wishing to travel to a brighter new world."
— Yvonne Yen, Double Diamond Director, USA

"This is the book that demonstrates the saying, 'Tough times don't last, tough people do!' Randy Ray's rags to riches account of his life's journey comes straight from the heart."
— Jirath Submongkonkul, Double Diamond Director, Thailand

"Randy shares his secrets of success with one great tale after another. An example for everyone to follow. This is one of those books you don't want to put down."
— Ming Lee, Double Diamond Director, USA

"We loved reading Randy's words of wisdom and gaining a greater appreciation of his unwavering spirit and commitment to make a difference in his life and the lives of others. The world is a better place with Randy Ray in it."
— Stefanie Nichols and Steve Green, Diamond Directors, USA

"I'm so glad that Randy has finally written the book so many people wanted him to write. He's a role model for every aspiring entrepreneur. And this is a wonderful, motivational read."
— Wai Chu Cheng, Diamond Director, Hong Kong

"If you know Randy, you already love him. If you don't know him, after reading this book you will love him like everyone else does because you will know him to be a successful, honest, upright and, most of all, loving man."
— Miguel Jaramillo, Double Diamond Director, Ecuador

"Reading about Randy's life brought tears to my eyes. His determination to rise above his poor childhood and his dream to help others is truly inspirational. *Mud Pies to Blue Skies* is a book that will change lives."
— Sannie Nie, Double Diamond Director, Canada

"The most beautiful and memorable journey in life is to follow Randy and his charitable work around the world. We loved reading about his struggles and successes and especially learning more about the poor children and villages Jeunesse Kids has supported."
— Hsin Yi Huang (Stacey) and Tser-Fu Chen (Jeff),
Double Diamond Directors, Taiwan

"Outstanding! Randy's story resonates with me. He's a man with a giant-size heart who helps those who suffer because he suffered himself. If you want to succeed, read this book and learn how to serve others."

— Oleg Permyakov, Diamond Director, Russia

"As a source of inspiration and joy, there's no one quite like Randy Ray. Randy's desire to contribute and his love for people comes through loud and clear. *Mud Pies to Blue Skies* is entertaining and informative, but most of all, it is motivating."

— Caio Carneiro, Double Diamond Director, Brazil

"Randy's success is an amazing achievement. What I admire most is his resilience, passion, dedication to make a difference in people's lives, and contagious positivity. It's all here in a book full of lessons from his life. Read it and you'll see what I mean."

— Fernão Basttistoni, Double Diamond Director, Brazil

"In a page-turner memoir, Randy Ray reveals how he used all the odds stacked against him as a reason to succeed instead of as an excuse to fail. His down-to-earth account shows how there is no straight line to success. It's a roller-coaster ride ultimately worth the journey."

— Calvin Becerra, Double Diamond Director, USA

"Randy is one of the happiest and funniest people I have ever met, and he has a huge heart. His dynamic and impish personality is on full display in this highly readable account of his life. What a legacy this man has created!"

— Marcus Clemente, Double Diamond Director, Brazil

"Randy has always dreamed big, sharing his vision and giving hope to people across the world. A true fighter against adversity and a respected role model, his enthusiasm and passion are clearly shown in the pages of this book."

— Roger Lin, Double Diamond Director, Taiwan

"You will love this book. You will love Randy. It will change who you are. Randy's story will pierce your heart and soul and give you the courage to go after what you want in life. He has created a legacy that will continue for generations."

— Ian and Judy Murray, Emerald Directors, Canada

"Life with Randy is never boring. *Mud Pies to Blue Skies* should become a family heirloom. It is a model for how to leave Earth better than you found it. Randy is a true living hero."

— Irawan Prajogo, Double Diamond Director, Indonesia

MUD PIES

—— *to* ——

BLUE SKIES

THE COLORFUL LIFE OF
RANDY RAY

MUD PIES
—— *to* ——
BLUE SKIES

THE COLORFUL LIFE OF
RANDY RAY

RANDY RAY

Jeunesse Kids Foundation, Inc., Lake Mary, Florida

Mud Pies to Blue Skies:
The Colorful Life of Randy Ray
by Randy Ray

ISBN: 978-1-953013-00-2 (hardcover)
ISBN: 978-1-953013-01-9 (paperback)

Published by

Jeunesse Kids Foundation, Inc., Lake Mary, Florida

Production: Malcolm Nicholl/The Balustrade Network,
www.thebalustradenetwork.com
Edited by Melanie Mulhall, Dragonheart
Interior layout by NZ Graphics, www.nzgraphics.com

First Edition

Printed in the United States of America

For Wendy, who lights my fire every day.

Contents

Foreword

By Craig Kielburger, WE Charity

Ifirst met Randy at a Jeunesse event, one of those stadium-sized conventions with lighting rigs and headset mics. It was held at a sprawling venue, the kind needed to contain the scale and energy that Randy and his family have built into the company. Randy was clad in a suit and tie, and he was a commanding presence, seated at his table with an entourage of hovering colleagues who were full of nervous excitement, brandishing cameras for photo ops. Randy, Wendy, and Scott were treated like celebrity guests, and yet they were gracious, careful to take time with each person. Well, at least that's when I first saw him. I only met him, really and truly, sometime later.

We were on a bus traversing a bumpy dirt road en route to the tiny village of Dao Lazui in rural China. Between the altitude and the time of year, it was bitterly cold out and everyone was shivering. Randy kept removing his coat and offering it to others, saying he was warm enough, making jokes about his waistline retaining all the heat. It was a small gesture that spoke to his incredible generosity and his instinct to put others first.

We were on a volunteer trip with a group of Jeunesse distributors, something that not every corporate leader would organize. But Randy and Wendy wanted their team to get their hands dirty, helping to lay bricks for a WE Charity classroom and meeting the children who would sit under its roof, some receiving a formal education for the first time thanks to this new school.

I watched Randy with a group of local kids. They were hesitant at first, shy around this new stranger with his imposing presence, deep voice, and accent they'd never heard before. As the partnership between WE Charity and Jeunesse grew, this would be a sight I saw repeated in all corners of the world. Randy and Wendy supported other villages in China, India, Ecuador, and Kenya and visited many of them. Wherever he landed, Randy would take up a chair and let kids gather around him to ask those curious and probing questions that only children can get away with. He would chuckle and joke with them, and he would tell them his own story, one of adversity and strength. It's the story you're about to read here.

Through a translator, Randy would tell the kids how, when he was their age, growing up in Tennessee, he made mud pies to eat, hoping that soil from the American South would dull the pains of his empty stomach. "I know what it means to be hungry," he would say. "And I know what it means to turn your life around." He would tell them he'd come so they could turn their lives around too.

Randy, Wendy, and Jeunesse Kids have since supported numerous classrooms (the ones in Dao Lazui have a heating system for those cold days), as well as libraries, teachers' accommodations, handwashing stations, immunizations, and countless other initiatives to give children a chance to turn their lives around, to give them access to clean water, food security, education, and health care, the tools they need to lift themselves out of poverty and to unleash their potential. The mission statement for his nonprofit, Jeunesse Kids, says everything: "Empowering communities to give children a brighter future."

Many companies create wealth and become successful in the traditional sense. Jeunesse Global is undoubtedly successful, one of the top-tier direct selling companies in the world. But for Randy, Wendy, and Scott, success means more than that. It means instilling everything they do, from business to philanthropy, with strong family values. And it means sharing opportunities with those who are often forgotten, especially young people. I can't think of a better symbol of that commitment than the WE College of Entrepreneurship in Kenya, funded by the Jeunesse community. The school will help kids in rural Kenya identify business prospects in their own communities so they can become leaders and entrepreneurs in their own right. These are kids who, like Randy, won't have anything handed to them. Instead, they need someone to believe in them so they can reach out and seize an opportunity of their own. It will teach financial literacy and instill in them a positive attitude toward self-employment. It will teach the next generation the skills that Randy demonstrated over the course of his incredible career rise from humble beginnings—the vision and tenacity he used to pull himself up by the bootstraps.

It's easy to see Randy as a suit and tie, a formidable business leader. But in my mind, to know Randy is to watch the man in an elementary classroom chair, surrounded by kids who sit rapt at his story as tears well up in his eyes, talking about mud pies and blue skies.

I know you'll get to meet Randy, really and truly, in these pages.

Craig Kielburger

Craig Kielburger
Cofounder, WE Charity

Introduction

We have been blessed, and our greatest joy is being able to share that blessing with others.

Iwas brought to tears by a little girl in a remote village in northeastern China. She stood up in a classroom we'd built in the village of Dao Lazui and in a confident voice, through a translator, she told my wife Wendy and me, "We're going to make you proud."

She was just eleven years old and grateful that her impoverished village had a new school with desks for each student and a library full of books. She was thrilled to have books.

I stood there as tears trickled down my cheeks, and I didn't care who saw them. It was an emotional moment for me, the realization of a dream to help kids who had been born into dire circumstances, as I had been many years before.

It was a moment more meaningful to me than the day I won a contract worth close to a billion dollars to develop a launch system for the Space Shuttle program or the day our company, Jeunesse Global, achieved one billion dollars in annual sales for the first time.

Seeing the joy on that young girl's face and hearing her heartfelt words of appreciation for the gift of learning were validation of my life's journey.

From a humble upbringing in rural Tennessee to building a business that has achieved billion-dollar sales five years in a row has been quite a trip.

I know what it's like to live in a shack with no electricity or running water, to work in a cotton field at the age of six, to be so hungry I ate mud pies while dreaming of a life where food and a comfortable bed would not be regarded as luxuries.

I was only fourteen when I sat by the side of a creek and scribbled six goals on a scrap of paper. Some of them were modest, like getting enough food to eat and new clothes to wear. Others were on a grander scale: to become a millionaire by the time I was thirty-five and to travel the world.

I'm proud to have achieved all six goals and even more proud to have helped many others achieve their financial goals. But best of all, my success has enabled me to give a hand up to children and their parents across the world who were born into abject poverty, efforts that have been selflessly supported by many of our 675,000 distributors across more than 145 countries.

Achieving my goals didn't come easy.

After leaving home at the age of sixteen with less than two dollars in my pocket, I slept in a cardboard box next to a dumpster and took whatever work I could find to feed and clothe myself. The US Army became my passport to an education and my first encounters with other cultures.

An aptitude for computer science was my springboard to success in the military and civilian life. After working for major corporations, I forged my own destiny and worked for myself, and in a David versus Goliath competition against major aerospace corporations, I landed the NASA account by developing breakthrough software. I ventured into creating and marketing medical software, which is how I met Wendy, my partner in everything, the love of my life, who makes my life complete.

We do everything together.

We've built three companies that were honored on the *Inc. 500* list of fastest growing privately owned businesses in America. Our experience in the network marketing industry is as multifaceted as it gets. We've worked as distributors, and we've run a business that provided all the back-office support for numerous network marketing startups. We built an international network marketing company of our own.

Then the pinnacle of our journey: Jeunesse Global.

It has been a phenomenal experience with rapid growth rarely enjoyed by any company. We couldn't have done it without our family of distributors across the globe who we love to visit and hear their success stories.

We have been blessed, and our greatest joy is being able to share that blessing with others—people like that little girl in Dao Lazui and other kids and their families we support in villages in Kenya, India, and Ecuador. We've helped them and so many more in many other countries through the nonprofit foundation we started, Jeunesse Kids. By purchasing this book, you have also contributed, because all of the proceeds go to the foundation.

I was inspired to write my life story following innumerable requests from distributors who heard me speak at events in country after country, who only knew part of the tale and clamored to know more. So here it is, by popular request, as they say. I hope you find my story uplifting and motivating; perhaps informative and educational. It shows how a boy who was so hungry he ate mud pies can, against all the odds and with grit and determination, soar into blue skies.

If nothing else, I pray it encourages you to make the most of the opportunities that come your way to live life to the fullest.

Chapter 1

You Have No Idea Who I Am

"When we leave this place, we're going to be accountable for two things: how we treated Mother Earth and how we treated the people on Earth."

I came into the world in a hurry, and I've been in a hurry ever since. I was born in a cotton field in rural Tennessee. Heavily pregnant, my mama was vigorously chopping cotton when she collapsed to the ground, felled by sudden, sharp labor pains. I like to say that I decided it was time to get out of the place where there were no lights and I had no one to play with. I couldn't wait any longer. Lying in the dirt among the rows of cotton, my mom had to deliver me all by herself. No one was in sight to help her give birth and welcome me into the world.

We lived way out in the boonies, and there was never a thought of going to a hospital for something as routine and as natural as childbirth. In 1941, especially in the countryside, kids were often born at home—although not usually alone and unattended in a field.

My mom named me Ogale Erandal Ray. Not the most common of names. And as the years went by, I got tired of people asking me how in the world I acquired such an unusual name. I'd say, "My mom gave it to me. She didn't ask my opinion." Where did my mom get it from? It beats the hell out of me, but to make it easier for everyone, I dropped Ogale and took Randy from my middle name, Erandal. I've been Randy Ray ever since.

My rustic birth occurred in an unremarkable dot on the map in McNairy County, Tennessee, called Gravel Hill, named after the hills in the area comprised of pea gravel that was used to pave highways. Other than that, Gravel Hill's only claim to fame is the cult classic Walking Tall, a movie loosely based on Sheriff Buford Puser, a no-nonsense professional wrestler who went to war with the local moonshiners.

My father never went to school a day in his life. He never learned to read or write, but he was part Cherokee Indian and possessed a lot of native wisdom. My mother was also part Indian, either Choctaw or Blackfoot. She never told me, but that's the best I could figure out from talking to relatives. Mom had an eighth-grade education but made us kids promise that we would finish twelfth grade.

My dad's name was Johnnie Ray, plain and simple. My mother's name was a bit more elaborate: Daisy Hazel Esther Lee Patmon Ray. Her folks threw in the names of her grandparents as well as an uncle and an aunt just to make them all feel good. I never knew any of my grandparents. They all died before I was born. It was such a hardscrabble life, it's not surprising they didn't live much beyond their forties and fifties.

My family was dirt poor. We were sharecroppers, which meant we worked on someone else's land and used their equipment. In return, we got a roof over our heads and a small share of the crop we produced.

When I was six, I was sent into the fields to plow with a mule. Even fully stretched, my little arms were barely able to reach the plow handles. I used a one-horse turning plow. You drove one mule down a line to turn the soil and then came straight back in the other direction.

It was tough work for an adult, never mind a child. And if I didn't plow straight lines, I got my ass whipped.

We all worked in the cotton fields: my mom and dad, my older brother JR, and later my younger brother, Winfred Alton, nicknamed Turkey because he was born on Thanksgiving. Even at the age of six, if I didn't pick a hundred pounds of cotton a day, it was another cause for an ass whipping. A hundred pounds is a lot of cotton. My fingers bled from the burrs sticking to them. My mama could pick three hundred pounds a day by tackling two rows at a time. I could only manage one row.

I tried a few creative ways to make the cotton I picked weigh more, like hiding a clod of dirt in the bottom of the sack. Once I peed on the cotton, convinced it would add to the weight. But at the end of the day, my dad noticed that the cotton was stained yellow. The jig was up. I got a whipping for that too. There were plenty of whippings to go around.

I was a scrawny kid with long, raggedy hair, bleached snow-white from being in the sun all the time. It earned me the nickname *Cottontop.*

There was never enough to eat, and we were always hungry. My little brother and I desperately scrounged through garbage dumps for scraps of food. We even ate patties made of mud—kind of like hamburger patties, but without the meat. When your stomach is racked with hunger pangs, believe me, you'll eat anything. Once in a while we'd get lucky and find a worm buried in the mud.

I wore threadbare clothes that people had thrown away, and I had to go barefoot most of the time, even in the winter when there was frost on the ground. My dad wrapped my feet in potato sacks or burlap bags, but that wasn't much protection against the rain and the snow. Water soaked right through the bags. My dad foraged through garbage dumps and sometimes found a soleless shoe that someone had discarded. He'd uncover something else to fashion the sole and hook rings to clasp the top and bottom together. My toes are all curled today because of those makeshift shoes, and I lost some feeling in my feet because of the frostbite.

I never had any toys, not even at Christmas. I never had a bicycle like other kids. I had to walk everywhere. One of my earliest memories is of an unusual act of kindness on a cold, rainy day when I was about nine. I stood in the mud waiting for the bus to arrive, having walked a mile or so in my bare feet to get to the bus stop. A lady who lived nearby, Mrs. Cole, Juanita Cole, saw me shivering, took pity on me, and called me into her house.

"I have a sausage biscuit left over from breakfast if you want it," she told me.

My folks may have been poor, but they had their pride and warned us not to accept food from people. We weren't beggars, they said. So I politely declined.

"I'm going to throw it out if you don't take it," she insisted. It was a white lie. It wasn't leftover food at all. I was so hungry I was only too happy to go along with the pretense.

Then Mrs. Cole made me sit down and disappeared, returning a little later with a pan of warm water. Crouching before me, she washed and dried my muddy feet. She cut the strap off a pair of her daughter's patent leather Easter shoes and tucked a pair of frilly white anklets inside so they fit better. I went to school wearing girls' shoes, but at least they were real shoes.

Years later, I told her daughter Betty, who is still a dear friend of mine, "Betty, I'm sorry I stole your shoes. I never did replace them."

The shabby clothes, the lack of shoes, and my overall scrawny and scruffy appearance made me a ripe target for the school bullies. For years, they ridiculed me, taunting and teasing me mercilessly. Once they stripped my overalls off me and left me lying naked in the hallway. Often, they chased my little brother and me in their pickup truck and beat the shit out of us. After one vicious attack, I peed blood for days.

From the time I was born until I left home at the age of sixteen, we never lived in a place that was livable. During those years we must have moved sixteen or seventeen times from one ramshackle, falling down property to the next. Our homes were wooden shacks with no insulation. Some had no windows, so we filled the spaces with cardboard to provide a measure of protection against the elements. In the dead of winter, if it was five below zero (Fahrenheit) outside, it was five below zero inside.

I like to say we were a very close family because three of us slept in one bed and three in the other, huddled together for warmth beneath old well-worn quilts. Our pillows were stuffed with sage grass that we collected from nearby fields. It was nowhere near as comfortable as down—not that I knew what down was back then. Lying there in the cold, I flinched as rats scurried over me and chewed off strands of my hair—material to help them construct their nests. Once, a particularly aggressive rat bit a plug out of my little brother's ear.

It was a horrible way to live. I craved something better, a whole lot better.

The floors in these homes were wooden planks, and through the cracks we could see our dogs and chickens running around in the dirt scrabble beneath the house. There was no electricity or running water. Everywhere we lived, Dad seemed to divine where we could find water, either a spring or a creek, and we had to haul buckets of water back to the house for drinking and cooking every day. We never had a bathroom. We didn't even have an outhouse. We pooped in the woods.

We cooked on a wood-burning stove and to keep warm, we burnt wood in the fireplace. From the time I was nine until I graduated high school, my job at bedtime was to cover up the fire with ashes. In the morning, I'd squat by the cold fireplace freezing my ass off to get the fire going again while everyone else was still in bed.

We were mostly self-sufficient. We had to be. We survived living off the land, and Dad took us fishing to catch something to eat. He'd gut the fish, clean it out, roll it in mud balls, and cook it on an open fire. After the fire burned down, he let the mud balls cool before cracking them open. Inside, all the scales and bones would have stuck to the mud, leaving the white meat for us to eat.

Us kids supplemented our diet by scouring the woods for anything edible that grew wild like huckleberries, muscadines, and poke. Poke sprouted on the creek banks. It tasted like spinach, but you had to be careful. When it produced berries, it became poisonous. At home we grew all kinds of vegetables and canned them.

We had chickens that laid eggs every day and cows we milked for buttermilk and butter. At any given time, we had five or six piglets, which we sold for cash or swapped for some commodity we needed. Dad killed a hog every year and placed the meat into a big box filled with salt so it would cure and last the rest of the year.

My mom and dad had completely different personalities. They say opposites attract, and that must have been true in their case. Dad was a saint, a gentle spirit who avoided conflict. This dude just flowed through life. Nothing bothered him. He didn't get upset. He didn't stomp around and yell.

My mom *did* get bothered and *did* yell—a lot. She was not at all affectionate, maybe because of the hard life we led or maybe because she wanted to toughen me up. I don't know. She beat our asses all the time, whipping us with a switch until blood ran down our legs.

I'd cry, "Mom, why are you whipping me?"

"You know why. You know," she'd reply.

I didn't know what I'd done wrong because more often than not, I hadn't done *anything* wrong. She just thought I deserved to be punished.

She was tough on my dad as well and bossed him around. "Johnnie, get a switch and whip that young'un's ass," she'd demand at times.

My dad pretended to whip me. I wore baggy overalls, and he made me arch my back so he hit the clothing instead of me. He'd whisper, "Yell 'Oh! Oh! Oh!' as if I'm hurting you." I'd scream in mock pain. But he never touched me, never hurt me at all.

He was such a tenderhearted person, he was even tender when he killed the hog every year. He sat down with the hog and fed it shelled corn, talking to it in a language I couldn't understand.

Once, I asked my cousin Billy what he was saying.

"He's telling the hog in Cherokee that we appreciate the sacrifice it is making for our sake," Billy explained.

Before the hog knew what was happening, Dad hit it hard with a sledgehammer right between the eyes and quickly cut its throat. The hog didn't have time to squeal. Then Dad strung it up. It was amazing how he did that, and it was such a compassionate thing to do.

We never owned any land. My dad didn't understand how you could own Mother Earth, a mindset that must have come from his Indian heritage. "You can't take it with you when you leave," he'd say. "We're just passing through, taking care of it while we're here."

We lived in five or six places in McNairy County before moving to the Tom Williams place. That's the way homes were identified in that part of the country back then. Homes were known by the names of the owner. After the Tom Williams place, we moved to the Mary Watkins place, the Charlie Curtis place, the Trim Mills place, the Burton Jones, the Dexter Stewart, and the Mason Brant. We paid rent, but it was never more than five dollars a month, so you can imagine what dumps they were.

The Tom Williams place was decent compared to all the others, but one day when the skies darkened and rain threatened, Dad hurriedly pitchforked loose hay into a wagon and severely ruptured himself. He was injured so bad he couldn't work, and because the house went with the job, they threw us out and moved a family that could work into the house. But they allowed us to sleep in the barn with the cows and the mules. Winter was approaching, and we plugged the cracks in the barn walls with cotton and anything else we could find in a futile attempt to stop the wind from blasting in. It was a brutal winter, and it was a miracle we didn't die because we all got sick. But we made it through and moved on to the next place.

For a few years, everything went to hell. My dad was crippled with arthritis of the spine and couldn't work at all. Hunched over, he limped along with the support of a walking stick. My brother JR, who was nine years older than me, did most of the work, earning enough to put food on the table. He helped raise us, and had it not been for him, we wouldn't have made it.

My father was often screwed over by people who took advantage of his lack of education, his part-Indian heritage, and his handicap. One day when I was about eleven or twelve, my dad and I walked through the town of Middleton. As he hobbled past the pool hall, some creeps sitting outside tripped him up. They laughed themselves stupid as my dad lay on the sidewalk, his head bleeding. I wondered how anyone could be so cruel and cried my eyes out as I tried to lift him to his feet. He was just minding his own business. You'd think my dad would have been really pissed, but he wasn't. He accepted it. We were just passing through. We didn't have a permanent place on the planet. What happened, happened.

Although my dad had no schooling, he demonstrated wisdom in many ways. One lesson he taught me early was that you can't un-ring a bell that has been rung. That was brought home to me after I got in trouble at school for hitting a little kid in the back of the head with a rubber bat. I don't think I had a good reason for doing it. Maybe I did it because Wayne's ears stuck out. Maybe I was bored. I don't remember. I do remember being taken to the principal, who gave me a paddling. At home that night, I complained to my dad, but he wasn't in the least sympathetic. "You shouldn't have done that," he said as he handed me a hammer and ordered me to drive a nail into a fence post.

Puzzled, I did what he instructed, and as I gave the hammer back to him, I asked, "Now what?"

"Let me know when you've apologized to the kid," he replied. "Then we'll take the nail out."

I had no idea what that was all about and thought about it for days until I realized that hitting Wayne was a terrible thing to have done. I had no cause to hit that kid. So I apologized to him. Wayne said it didn't bother him at all, which made me real happy, and I rushed home to tell my dad.

"Go pull the nail out," he demanded. Then he had me hand it to him. "What's left there in the fence post?"

"The hole where the nail was," I said, thinking that the answer was pretty obvious.

"That's right," my dad said. "Remember, you can hurt someone and you can apologize, but you can never fill in that hole. You can never undo what you did."

He couldn't read or write, but he was full of wise observations like that.

There was a guy named Oscar Cole who was just as kind as his wife Juanita, the lady who'd fed me breakfast and given me her daughter's shoes. Mr. Cole let us use some of his land for free and even offered to carry our crop at no cost to the cotton gin where the cotton fiber was separated from seeds, dirt, and stems. While my dad couldn't work, my mom, JR and I, at the age of eleven or twelve, threw ourselves into the task.

We produced three bales of cotton, the best crop ever, and the beauty of it was we didn't have to share it with anybody. Mr. Cole hauled it to the cotton gin, which was owned by a Mr. Shelley, who also ran the dry goods store where we'd been given credit to buy seed and fertilizer. My dad stood as straight as he could, resting on his cane, proud as a peacock of the job his family had done. We expected to collect a pile of cash for our labors, but Mr. Shelley didn't see it that way and tried to swindle us.

He weighed the cotton, pretended to do a calculation, and declared, "Mr. Ray, we just about came out even here. Get your boys a pair of overalls and we'll call it even."

He knew my dad couldn't read and he took advantage of him. It took all the life out of my dad.

As young as I was, I didn't want to let this man get away with it. I tried to intervene. "You're cheating my dad."

Mr. Shelley looked down his nose at me and said scathingly, "Boy, you're getting above your raising. You don't talk to me like that. I'm Mr. Shelley."

He made it clear that he was somebody and we were nobodies; that he was above us and we needed to know our place in the world. He booted us out of the store.

We had to endure that kind of thing a lot, and I like to think there are front row seats in hell reserved for people like that.

My dad didn't deserve to be so dishonored and disrespected. He was one of the most caring individuals you could ever encounter. One thing he said a lot was, "When we leave this place, we're going to be accountable for two things: how we treated Mother Earth and how we treated the people on Earth."

And he practiced what he preached.

Everywhere we lived, my dad tried to stop erosion. He'd cut a cedar tree and place it in the ditch where soil was eroded. He'd also dig up the saplings of an apple tree or a peach tree and take them with us to plant in the yard of the next house.

"Dad, why do you do that?" I asked after he had done this several times. "We never stay anywhere long enough to get fruit from any of these trees."

He looked at me as if I were crazy, "Well, the people who follow us will."

I was thinking of myself; he was taking a worldview.

I was about eight when he taught me a lesson about the generosity of the human spirit. A family of black sharecroppers that lived near us had a whole bunch of little kids. Their dad, Ted Damons, got really ill and couldn't work. Without hesitation, my dad stepped in to help. He lined us up and marched us single file over to their farm. We milked the cows, slopped their hogs, took eggs into their house, and did all kinds of jobs.

"Dad, why are we over here doing all this work?" I asked.

"We may need his help someday," he replied.

"Do you think he would help us?"

"I think he would, but if he wouldn't, that's his problem, not mine."

This is the kind of lesson you never forget, and it has stuck with me. It's lessons like this that I've had the good fortune to share with hundreds of thousands of people around the world.

I got a different kind of lesson from my mother. Education was important to her, and before I was old enough to start school, she drilled me on the ABCs and multiplication tables, even though we had no books at home. True to form, she was strict. If I screwed up and couldn't get the multiplication correct—seven times five equals thirty-five, for instance—I didn't get to eat. I have distaste for math to this day.

My first school was in Acton, Tennessee, but then we moved. We were always moving. I went to a one-room schoolhouse where the teacher, Burnett North, taught all eight grades. There were no more than thirty of us. Later, when we lived near Pocahontas, Tennessee, I attended school in Middleton. I started in second grade, but after a week, they advanced me to the third grade because I was no dummy.

As I mentioned, my mom made it to the eighth grade but made us kids promise we'd finish twelfth grade. For her, that was the epitome of a successful education. I'm sure she'd be doing somersaults in her grave if she knew how much I've accomplished. But she was incapable of showing love. I used to beg her to tell me she loved me. For whatever reason, she wouldn't or couldn't.

"Mom, I don't care if you love me or not, I love me and I'm going to be somebody," I said to her when I was fourteen. "I'm going to do great things, and nothing's going to stop me."

Then I went down to the creek and sat on the bank. With the stub of a pencil, I wrote out all the goals I intended to achieve on a yellow sheet of notepaper.

The first item on the list, and the most aspirational, was to become a millionaire by the time I was thirty-five. I picked thirty-five because

Jimmy Simpson, the local banker's son, was thirty-five. I figured he wasn't a millionaire, but he was in the banking business, so he had to be making big money. When you think about it, it was laughable because I didn't have two nickels to rub together.

The second thing I wrote in my childish scrawl was to get enough food to eat every day because I was starving all the time.

Third was new clothes—my own clothes, not third-hand shirts and pants that didn't fit.

Fourth was to acquire a car. We never owned a car, and I was determined to have a vehicle of my own.

Fifth was to live in a house that had electricity, something else I'd never enjoyed.

Sixth was travel. I'd not even been as far as the county line, but I knew I wanted to travel all over the world. I wanted to learn about other people from other cultures, understand what made them tick, and find out what was important to them. I don't know where the desire to travel and get to know people from other cultures came from, but I was always curious about how other people lived.

I finished writing the list, carefully folded the sheet of paper, and tucked the paper into my pants pocket. For years, I unfolded it and refolded it, reading it and rereading it, until eventually, it fell apart. It didn't matter. Those goals were indelibly burned into my mind. Nobody could take them out of my head. Come hell or high water, that's what I was going to do. I believed with all my heart and soul that I was going to achieve those goals.

Most of the goals were modest by most people's standards, but not by mine. And with God's help, I accomplished them all. I even surpassed the goal of becoming a millionaire by the time I was thirty-five—the biggest goal—when I was thirty-two and collected a check for six million dollars.

My mother did teach me one valuable lesson about the same time when I made that list, and it was something more like what my dad would say than what she usually said. It was her response to my asking why we were so poor.

"We're not poor, we're broke," she said. "Poor is a state of mind. If you think you're poor, you'll be poor all your life. Broke is temporary. We can always get money somewhere."

I was determined to get money anywhere and any way I could, and I could be very creative. When a new Baptist preacher came to town and asked me if I wanted to make a dollar, I displayed my entrepreneurial flair for the first time. Of course I wanted to make a dollar. My whole life was about trying to make a living. His garden was threatened by being overrun with nut grass, and he wanted it removed. I was up for that. He gave me a large box to cart off the nut grass, and then I had a brilliant idea. There were a lot of homes with gardens in a row along a back alley, so I went house to house, throwing the nut grass over the walls into their yards until I ran out of it.

Two weeks later, after it had rained and I knew the nut grass would have taken hold, I went door-to-door.

"Do y'all have a nut grass problem," I asked. "The preacher did, and he paid me a dollar to get rid of it all."

And wouldn't you know, they did have a nut grass problem, and ten families were happy to pay me a dollar to get rid of it. That was one inspired way to turn a dollar job into a ten-dollar job. You create a need and you fill it!

I took to heart what my daddy said: "If there's anything you want in life, you got to go out and work for it. Nobody on this planet owes you anything."

Selling newspapers was a more regular gig. A weekly newspaper called *Grit*, which claimed to be "America's Greatest Family Newspaper," was very popular in rural America. I walked all over town each week selling it for ten cents, and four cents was mine to keep.

I picked blackberries from the hedgerows and sold buckets of them in town. The lady who managed the local train depot gave me picture postcards from a sack of the many she'd collected, and I went door-to-door selling picture postcards for a nickel each. At Christmas, I climbed trees to gather mistletoe and sold that as well.

I once went into a local beauty salon and offered to sweep out the floor or do anything else to make a few bucks. The owner wasn't interested, hit me in the ass with a broom, and chased me out the door. The beauty salon is still there, run by that lady's daughter. Ironically, they have Jeunesse products on the shelf.

I was a straight-A student until I got to the eighth grade when the teasing and bullying became so overwhelming. I lost interest and played hooky a lot. Even my older brother and his buddies picked on me.

Our favorite swimming hole was at the end of the cotton field. One blazing hot day I went for a swim to cool off before all the workers arrived, stripped buck naked, and jumped in. When I got out, my clothes had disappeared. As I frantically searched for them, I realized a dozen people picking cotton were approaching my end of the field. I had no choice other than to get back in the water and hide. By the time the workers were out of sight, I looked like a shriveled prune, much to the amusement of my older brother and his buddies, who showed up to return my clothes.

But they weren't done with me. I wanted to go with them. They agreed, but only if I peed on a little wire they pointed out to me. Assuming it was a test of my accuracy, I jumped on a tree stump and carefully aimed at the wire. I had no idea it was a live electric wire until it knocked me senseless. I ran home to tell my mom, and it was my brother who got the ass whipping that day.

Sadly, my relationship with my mother never improved. At the age of fifteen, I sat by her bedside as she died. I held her hand and begged her to tell me that she loved me, but she never did. It haunted me for years.

A few years ago, on a visit to the area where I'd grown up, my daughter Cynthia talked with one of my high school teachers, who told her how one of my pranks had infuriated her. "I was teaching my heart out, and Ogale crawled out of a window along the ledge on one side of the building and came back in through another window. I asked him a tough question, thinking I'd embarrass him in front of the class, but it backfired because he knew the answer. He always knew the answer!"

Many of the teachers looked down on me. To them, I was a nobody, a nothing. When I got to the twelfth grade and they took kids to check out various colleges, they were embarrassed by my appearance and wouldn't let me participate.

"You don't need to go," they said. "You know you're not going to college. You're going to work on a farm."

They had me pegged in a little box, and I wasn't going to accept that. "I'm not going to work on a farm. I've worked on a farm ever since I was born." As far as I was concerned, they had no idea where I was going.

And over the years, whenever people have doubted my abilities, I've thought *You have no idea who I am and where I'm going.*

Chapter 2

The Idiot in the Attic

I didn't know where I was going. I just knew I was going someplace to be somebody.

I left home the morning after I graduated from twelfth grade. I was sixteen.

I didn't tell anyone what I was going to do. I got up real early, squeezed my one change of clothes into a small bag my brother had brought back from the army, and slipped out of the house before anyone else was awake.

With less than two dollars in small change jingling in my pockets, I strode the five miles to the crossroads where highway 125 intersected highway 57, the highway that would take me straight into Memphis.

Optimistically, I stuck my thumb out and didn't have to wait long before a guy on his way home from a fishing trip pulled over. I'm sure he wondered what this baby-faced, skinny kid was doing hitchhiking all alone.

And he asked where I was going.

I didn't know where I was going. I just knew I was going someplace to be somebody.

I asked where he was heading.

He was going as far as Memphis, and that was fine with me. I'd never been to Memphis. Memphis was the big city. It wasn't much more than eighty miles away, but it was a world away from the life I'd led at home. I didn't know a single soul in Memphis. I had no place to live and no job to go to. But it would be the start of a new life, even if it was a giant step into the unknown.

I chewed this guy's ear off the whole way there. I don't remember what I talked about. I was just excited to have hit the road, leaving everything and everyone I'd ever known behind me. When we got to Memphis, the driver pulled over and told me, "This is where I turn off for my home. You have to get out here."

I hadn't a clue where "here" was. I scooted out of the car, thanked him for the ride, and wondered what I was going to do. I had no plan.

On the corner was a quick service restaurant housed in a small white brick cottage with a blue roof, one of many identical outlets in the national Toddle House chain. They were open twenty-four hours a day, seven days a week, but they specialized in breakfast. There were no tables, just a row of ten stools at a stainless steel counter. Customers paid their bill on the way out.

I ventured inside, helped myself to some packages of crackers that were sitting in a little straw basket, and energetically shook both mustard and ketchup onto the crackers. It wasn't much of a breakfast, but I was hungry and needed to get whatever calories I could. And it was free. I politely asked for a glass of water and got into conversation with the folks who worked behind the counter. I confessed my predicament to them: I didn't have any place to go.

Their only suggestion was to bed down for the night among a row of dumpsters lined up against a shed next door.

I found an empty refrigerator box, which became my bedroom, and set it up so the open part of the box (my door) was pressed against the shed wall, providing protection from the dogs that savaged the dumpsters at night. For the next four months, that was my home. Every day, wearing my work overalls, which was pretty much all I had to wear, I went door-to-door looking for work, any kind of work. Jobs were scarce, and no one wanted to hire a scrawny kid who looked like he still belonged in school.

I often went back into the Toddle House to dine on their crackers, mustard, and ketchup. One time they took pity on my sorry ass and offered me a burger they said had been dropped on the floor. I didn't care how much dirt it might have collected, and I quickly devoured it. After all, I'd eaten mud patties with my brother. But I also didn't believe they'd dropped the burger. They were just being kind.

I looked everywhere for a place to stay, and someone told me about a boarding house on Peabody Avenue. Before giving me a room, the old lady who ran the place asked what kind of job I had.

"Well, I don't have one right now, but I'm getting one," I told her, always the optimist.

She was adamant: if I couldn't pay, I couldn't stay. Day after day, I turned up on her doorstep. I asked if I could have a room if I cut the grass, raked the leaves, took out the trash, or did some other work for her. Anything.

"No. You must have money," she said.

I went back so many times she finally got tired of it and gave in. Kind of. She took me indoors and walked me up the stairs to the dusty third-floor attic. It was July and it had to be a blistering 150 degrees up there.

The room was bare except for an old army cot. A small dormer window opened to allow a gentle, merciful breeze, but still, it was baking hot. Nevertheless, I gratefully accepted the accommodation. I was happy to have a real roof over my head, a place where I didn't have to worry about mangy dogs sniffing around. It was a heck of a lot better than my cardboard refrigerator box.

Better than that, I had electricity for the first time in my life and access to a bathroom. The room had a single light, a bare bulb hanging from the ceiling with a cord attached. I lay on the bed the first night so mesmerized to have light that I tugged on the cord, turning the light on and off. It was a luxury to me, and I wrote home to tell them I was living upstairs in a big house with electric lights and a bathroom.

Now that I had a room, a bed, and access to a bathroom, my challenge was to find work so I could earn enough to feed myself.

One night after I'd been living there for a few weeks, I trudged back to the boarding house, exhausted and hungry. I walked enviously past the dining room where the paying guests were enjoying their evening meal.

Above the noise coming from the roomful of guys happily chowing down food I couldn't possibly afford, I heard someone ask, "Who's the idiot in the attic?"

They were talking about me. I was the idiot. I dejectedly dragged myself up the stairs and sat on the army cot. Resting my head in my hands, I thought about it for a long time. What the hell was I doing up there? Overhearing that conversation was my wake-up call. The realization that those guys thought I was an idiot gnawed at me. I redoubled my efforts to find work.

Eventually, I got a job as a plumber's helper, which was ironic considering that we'd never had plumbing at home, so I knew nothing about it. Regardless, I desperately needed a job and a regular paycheck, so when I saw the help wanted sign, I went for it.

"What kind of work have you done," the owner asked.

"Picking cotton and chopping cotton," I replied.

"How much they pay you?"

I answered honestly. "Three dollars per one hundred pounds of picking. Three dollars a day for chopping."

"Do you have a driver's license?"

"Yes," I replied proudly. Luckily, even though my family never owned a car, I'd taken driver's ed at school and passed the test the first time I took it. I was the proud possessor of a Tennessee driver's license.

"Okay," he said. "You got the job."

I was so excited I didn't ask any questions. I didn't even ask how much I was getting paid.

The guy screwed me. He paid me three dollars a day, the same as I'd earned slaving in the cotton fields. In spite of that, I continued to work my ass off to prove I was a reliable, capable employee. The work was as tough as the cotton fields. Manfully operating a jackhammer that weighed more than me, I cracked open concrete so trenches could be dug to install sewer lines.

At the end of the week, tired but satisfied that I'd done a good week's labor, I collected my pay. It was all of eighteen dollars. Damn, I thought. That's not a lot of money for all the work I've done. After about three weeks of this, I was in conversation with another worker who was moaning about deductions from his paycheck, and I found out exactly how much I'd been screwed. While I'd been paid eighteen dollars a week, he'd been paid more than one hundred dollars. I was pissed. Immediately, I drove the old Ford panel truck back to the shop, marched into the owner's office, and threw the keys on his desk.

"What are you doing?" he demanded.

"I quit," I said.

"Why?"

"You know why," I angrily told him. "You worked me like a dog. You screwed me."

I walked out of my first real job.

I looked for other work, willing to do anything. For a while, I pumped gas at a Gulf service station. Then I got a job as a stock boy at the Lowenstein's department store on Main Street, but stacking rugs played havoc with my hay fever, and I quit. As luck would have it, I got into conversation with a lady I bumped into at the Toddle House restaurant across the street from the store. For some reason, she took a shine to me and offered to introduce me to the owner of the Pic Pac supermarket. She even took me to buy a pair of khaki pants and a white shirt so I'd look presentable and went with me on the bus to Lamar-Airways Shopping Center for the interview. I got the job.

At first, I bagged groceries and carried them out to customers' cars. I have to say, I did a really good job. That was the way I operated. No matter how menial the task I always put in a hundred percent effort. I was promoted to stockman, changing the prices on products, and that was quickly followed by a more responsible position as a relief cashier. With regular wages in my pocket and freedom I'd never experienced before, I began to sow a few wild oats. I was a teenager, after all.

My older brother didn't approve of my shenanigans and showed up unannounced on my doorstep. He barged into the house, grabbed me by the scruff of the neck, and made me pack some clothes. Then he dragged me out to his car and drove me to Walnut, Mississippi, where he lived and where he worked at a chemical plant. He recommended me for a position there, and because I'd done well in chemistry at school, they made me a lab technician. I tested plastic panels to make sure they were fireproof and affixed the underwriter seal of approval.

But I was restless. This wasn't the life I wanted. I envisioned a life in the army. In Memphis, I'd heard about a US Army program where they paid your way through college if you enlisted for a certain number of years. I knew I couldn't get far in life without a college degree, and there was no other way I could afford that kind of education. So I showed up at the local Memphis recruiting office, took the entrance test, and passed with flying colors. I knew that the future I wanted required an education, and the US Army was going to be my ticket to it.

But there were a few problems I had to overcome. The recruiters wanted to see my birth certificate, and they asked for the name of the hospital where I'd been born. I told them I didn't have a birth certificate and had been born in a field, not in a hospital. The recruiters had a hard time believing that I'd been born in a field, and there was no way to escape the requirement that I produce a birth certificate.

I had to scuttle around to get a birth certificate. George Whaley, our local mail carrier in Middleton, helped me fill out the application form for one. The questions would have been easily answered by most people, but they were anything but mundane for me, and I answered them to the best of my ability. Where was I born? A field. Who witnessed the birth? No one other than my mother, and she'd already passed on. What was the date of my birth? I didn't know for sure, so we put down the date I'd been told was my birthdate, May 21. We sent off the form to the records office at the state capital, Nashville, where it got stamped and approved.

There was another snag. Because I was only seventeen, the recruiters said that my parents needed to give their signed permission for me to enlist. The army was going to spend a lot of money on my education, and they needed some assurance I would honor the terms of the deal and stay in for the agreed time. I confessed that my mom wasn't around to sign because she'd passed on and that my daddy couldn't read or write and didn't know how to sign his name.

"You gotta be shitting me," said the recruiting sergeant. He'd never heard anything like it.

My older brother helped me out and brought my dad to the Memphis recruiting office so he could sign the paperwork—or at least make his mark with an X, which is what he usually did. The moment they placed the agreement in front of my dad, he looked at it and said, "Someone's already signed for me. Somebody's forged my name." He didn't know any better. He was so pure and innocent he'd looked at the X that indicated the line where the signature was to be made and thought someone had forged his signature. God, I loved him.

But that was it. He made a mark with his X, and I belonged to the US Army.

Chapter 3

The Military Man

I became obsessed with the computer science course probably because it was my passport to a new world.

I was sent to Fort Knox, Kentucky, known worldwide as the place where the US government stored billions of dollars of gold in an impenetrable vault. I wasn't there for the gold, although I would have happily accepted a couple of the twenty-seven-pound solid gold bars from the government's stash. Heck, I'd take just one, any day.

I was stationed next door at the Fort Knox Army Base for eight weeks of basic training. I completed that and had another eight weeks of advanced training—what they called MOS, Military Occupational Specialty. My "specialty" was administrative work: typing and filing; doing all kinds of not-so-exciting office stuff. I thought that would be my ticket to keep me out of jungles and deserts and far away from combat missions. I should have known better. Things in the army don't always work out the way you expect.

If I learned anything in Uncle Sam's army, it was to accept that hurry up and wait was the norm and that something unexpected is always waiting just around the corner. Usually something not too pleasant.

After initial training, I was assigned to an administrative post at the Fort Devens, Massachusetts, base. I wasn't sure what was going to happen to me or where I was going to be sent—this was the US Army after all—but I had to get a ton of security clearances: TS-ESI (Top Secret Exceptionally Sensitive Information); COSMIC Top Secret (Control of Secret Material in an International Command); Crypto clearance for cryptographic information on communications codes; and more. It was quite heady stuff for a teenager from the backwoods of Tennessee, and although I didn't know it, some of the clearances were required to work with people in international organizations like NATO (North Atlantic Treaty Organization) and SEATO (Southeast Asia Treaty Organization).

While based at Fort Knox, I met the girl who would become my first wife. I was only eighteen, and she was even younger. Younger than I knew. For some reason, her mom wanted us to get married in Mississippi. That was okay with me because my brother and his family lived there. I didn't realize I was like a lamb being led to the slaughter. It wasn't until all the families were assembled and we got the marriage license that I discovered she was only fifteen. Back then, Mississippi was one of a handful of states where you could get married that young with parental permission. That's the reason her mom wanted us to get married there. I really didn't know what I was doing. I was eaten up with a case of dumbass.

Seven days after the wedding, I shipped out to the Far East on a two-year deployment. It didn't last that long because my father had a heart attack and I got to come back early. But while I was gone, living on the other side of the world, my wife was at home spending all the money I sent her. We were both too young and inexperienced to be married, but we managed to hold things together for twenty years before we called it quits. While we had our ups and downs, she blessed me with three wonderful daughters who now have their own children who continue to make me a proud papa.

My first stop on my first journey outside the US was Tachikawa

Air Force Base in Japan, twenty miles outside Tokyo, which was basically a holding pen before being given a permanent assignment. I'd only been there a few days when I got a message that a general was coming to see me. Holy shit! I was a buck private. What did a general want with me? How did he even know I existed?

I got all dressed up for the occasion in my neatly pressed army uniform, shoes spit-shined, and jumped to attention when the general and his entourage strode into the barracks. The general walked up to me, walked around me, and circled a couple of times. I wondered what he was doing.

"At ease," he ordered.

Under those circumstances, being at ease was not easy.

"Do you play football?" he asked out of nowhere.

I had to admit I didn't. I was a poor country boy. At home, I never had a football or baseball to play with. I never played at school, either, because the other kids didn't want me on any of the teams. I was too scrawny, too weak. But my months in the army had turned me into a man. For the first time in my life I'd had three square meals a day: breakfast, lunch, and dinner. I'd run five miles a day, performed seemingly endless push-ups and sit-ups. I'd gained weight and I'd gained muscle. The army had whipped me into superb physical shape.

"You've got the right build," the general said. "You'll make a great football player. We'll train you."

This general wanted to win the Far East Division Championships against the other units, and he had me shipped over to South Korea to join KMAG, the Korean Military Advisory Group, whose role was to train and provide logistical support for the Republic of Korea Army.

My key job, said the general, would be to kill the quarterback. Of course, he didn't mean that literally, but I was tasked with neutralizing opposing quarterbacks. I did it quite effectively. I ripped up a few star quarterbacks, although I wound up having a few broken ribs of my own. The general obviously knew how to recruit talent. We won the championship.

My time in Korea was fascinating, especially when I was attached to the US Army Special Forces, the famous Green Berets.

In Korea, I got to mingle with people from many different countries and cultures, and I accomplished one of the main goals that the fourteen-year-old Randy had scrawled on that scrap of paper: to travel overseas and learn what made other people tick. One of the results of cultural mixing was affairs between Korean girls and American soldiers. Their offspring, mixed race babies, were scorned in Korean culture, and as they got a little older, the children were sometimes abandoned. You'd see these kids out on the streets crying, begging, and freezing to death, sometimes literally, in the brutally cold winters. You'd see someone throw money into a child's begging can and then someone else dart out of a back alley and steal the money. It tugged at my heartstrings.

I couldn't bear to see the children exist like that, shunned and abused. I thought about what we could do to help. At KMAG, we got a nurse from the national hospital to open an orphanage, and every payday, I encouraged everyone to contribute to help take care of the kids. Then we hit the streets looking for kids to take to the orphanage. We managed to rescue dozens of children and get them into a place where they had a comfortable bed and hot meals, but there wasn't much we could do about the widespread societal discrimination.

The college education the army had promised included core requirements through the University of Maryland's Far East Division campus. When I was first told I'd be going to the University of Maryland, I naively assumed classes would be somewhere in the state of Maryland. But that's not the way it worked. The army agreed to pay your way through college, but depending on where you were assigned, you might go to fifteen different colleges all over the world, gathering credits along the way. There were times I'd be in an area with a good school and could attend classes. In other places, I had to take a correspondence course.

After my time in South Korea, I returned to the States and was stationed at the Sixth US Army headquarters at the Presidio of San Francisco, which gave me the opportunity to attend San Francisco State. I was commander of the color guard for ceremonial occasions and parades. Talk about spit and polish. We wore chrome helmets, white gloves, white epaulettes, and white laces in our boots as we marched bearing Remington 6 rifles. In the evenings, I went to night classes and afterward pumped gas at a service station until midnight or later. After a few hours' sleep, I was back on duty at the base. That was my learn-and-earn routine for a couple of years.

But it wasn't all work. On weekends, I found time to party. I drank vodka like there was no tomorrow and smoked four packs of cigarettes a day. My apartment was party central until I came to my senses one night. In the middle of the night, in a drunken haze, I staggered into the bathroom. When I stared at myself in the mirror, I got a shock. I was haggard and disheveled. My eyes were two tiny angry slits staring back at me and my throat was raw and burning from the cigarette smoke.

As intoxicated as I was, I muttered to myself, "You can't do this anymore."

I wandered around the apartment, sidestepped all the bodies lying asleep everywhere, and gathered up all the booze and cigarettes—not just mine, everybody's. I took it all outside and threw it in the chute that went down to the dumpster. Back inside my apartment, I passed out. Later that morning, I was awakened by people screaming, wanting to know what had happened to their booze and cigarettes. I quit cold turkey that day. It was seven months before I had another drink, and even then, I only drank in moderation. I haven't smoked since.

Next stop was with the First Logistical Command at Fort Hood, Texas. That's when I met President Kennedy during his last full day in this world. We'd been sent on a training exercise to Fort Sam Houston in San Antonio, and while we were there, the president made a whistle-stop visit to the city to speak at the dedication ceremony for the Brooks Air Force Base Aerospace Medical Health Center. He took time to stop and shake our hands and tell us we were doing a great job. He was really proud of the Green Berets. Meeting him was a great moment. The next day, he went to Dallas. We heard the news as we were driving home.

The whole command was about to be sent to Parker, Arizona, for a ninety-day exercise—CPX Desert Strike, I believe it was called. The thought of sweating my ass off in hundred-degree heat had zero appeal to me. Fortunately, a guy at headquarters came to the rescue with an interesting option. He told me that the army was starting a new project, developing its own computer scientists instead of hiring expensive outside contractors. Why didn't I apply for that?

It wasn't as if I'd dreamed of becoming a computer scientist. I didn't know anything about computers. I'd never even seen a punch card for that matter. But for some reason, I was driven to do it, and not just because it was a way to avoid the desert exercise. Ever since I'd left home, I'd felt like God was directing me, and this was destined to be a life-transforming event. I filled out the paperwork, and within a day or two, I got my marching orders: You're in. Pack your bags. You're going to New Jersey.

Fort Monmouth, New Jersey, was the home of the US Army Signal

Corps, the unit in charge of the computer science project. As soon as I arrived, I was subjected to an entrance exam. The moment I sat down at the damn table and scanned through the questions, I knew I was in trouble. My lack of education was about to be exposed.

Many of the questions required a basic knowledge of algebra, geometry, and trigonometry—subjects I had avoided like the plague in high school. Not surprisingly, I flunked the test. Big time. The registrar told me I was out and had to return to my unit.

I begged him to let me stay—I mean, really begged. "Put me on probation," I pleaded. "I'll study harder than anyone you've ever met. I'll work around the clock." I did everything but get down on my knees and clasp my hands in prayer. I guess I was really persuasive. Amazingly, the registrar relented and allowed me to attend a crash course at the local high school to catch up on the math I needed to learn computer science. I didn't care that I was the oldest kid in the class. Without that knowledge, I was going nowhere fast. The next time I took the entrance exam, I sailed through it.

I was determined to succeed, which meant there was no time for fun. I didn't go out drinking with the guys. I didn't go out anywhere. I studied seven days a week, hunkered down in the computer lab hour after hour, and even slept in the lab a few nights. I had to prove to myself, as well as to the army, that I could do it. I was focused on excelling, determined to impress, and intent on getting qualified. It turned out that computer science was my thing.

I became obsessed with the computer science course, probably because it was my passport to a new world.

Not only did I get a bachelor's degree in computer science, but I also graduated number one with honors in my class of 104 students. On top of that, I obtained a bachelor's in psychology, a subject that fascinated the hell out of me because it provided meaningful insights into human behavior. It was like a thousand lights came on, brightly shining a new perspective on my personal life and family relationships.

I'd always hated the fact that my mother had never told me she loved me. I thought she'd been unusually cruel when she raised me, physically whipping me and verbally abusing me for no good reason that I could see. Lessons learned from the psychology course made me reconsider my attitude. Perhaps I didn't appreciate all the struggles she'd been through, the hardships she'd lived through. I came to the conclusion that she probably did the best she could with what she had. My studies in psychology allowed me to understand some of the things that had probably made my mom who she was, and I forgave her. I wished it had been possible to establish a better relationship with her before she died.

A book I read during this time, *The Prophet* by Kahlil Gibran, had a profound lifelong effect on me.

I memorized Gibran's famous poem "On Children" because its message resonated with me.

And a woman who held a babe against her bosom said,
Speak to us of Children.
And he said:
Your children are not your children.
They are the sons and daughters of Life's longing for itself.
They come through you but not from you,
And though they are with you yet they belong not to you.

You may give them your love but not your thoughts
For they have their own thoughts.
You may house their bodies but not their souls,

For their souls dwell in the house of tomorrow,
which you cannot visit, not even in your dreams.
You may strive to be like them, but seek not to make
them like you.
For life goes not backward nor tarries with yesterday.

You are the bows from which your children as living arrows
are sent forth.
The archer sees the mark upon the path of the infinite,
and He bends you with His might that His arrows may go
swift and far.
Let your bending in the archer's hand be for gladness;
For even as He loves the arrow that flies, so He loves also
the bow that is stable.

The point is, you don't really own anybody other than yourself. The book changed my whole outlook on life. It guided me to appreciate that parents often do the same stupid things to their kids that their parents did to them. We tend to play the parent tapes. In other words, learned behavior sticks with you. I hope that reaching that realization made me a better parent.

It's not only parents, of course, who help chart the course of your life. There were two professors who really lit my fire for learning: Dr. Faresse at the University of Maryland who said I had a very breezy style of writing reports and Dr. Bergman, head of the psychology department at San Francisco State. I'm forever in their debt.

Graduating first in my class had its advantages. General Paul D. Adams, a four-star army general and Commander-In-Chief, United States Strike Command (STRICOM), picked me to head his team of computer scientists at MacDill Air Force Base in Tampa, Florida.

STRICOM was a unified combatant command of all branches of the military tasked with responding to global crises. It was a plum assignment, and I went from freezing my ass off in New Jersey to experiencing the subtropical climate of central Florida.

One of my first projects was to set up a command and control system for generals and colonels, who knew nothing about computers and were probably not inclined to master the intricacies of such technological advances.

Our challenge was to design a way that they could walk up to a large computer console and access information by typing simple requests in plain English. We developed what was called Computer Control Language (CCL). For instance, an officer could enter "get airfield file," pull up all the specifications of particular airfields, and get answers to pertinent questions: Can you land a B52 bomber? Can the runway take a heavy plane like the C130 transport? Is the runway long enough for the F-4 Phantom jet? What is the surface of the runway, concrete or asphalt? What about fueling capabilities? What kind of navigational aids does it have? Lighting? Can planes fly in at night? There were many different factors that had to be taken into account. To make it even more idiotproof, we came up with a push-button system to access the information.

My team and I cracked it, so much so that I was called on to demo the system to Secretary of Defense Robert S. McNamara, who flew to MacDill with his team for the presentation. He was blown away by the fact that his own military people had developed the software, saving the Department of Defense the expense of hiring outside contractors.

The army continued to make good on its promise to give me a college education. I studied at the University of Tampa and even attended a systems design course at the prestigious Massachusetts Institute of Technology (MIT).

Attending MIT was an amazing experience. At its Lincoln Laboratory, I learned advanced systems design, programming on the IBM 1410 and then the 1440 models. My father couldn't read and write, but his son was taking classes with some really sharp people from all across the country, being trained by instructors who were nothing short of brilliant. And we got to work on computers that few people had ever worked on before. *I'm on my way,* I told myself. *Just wait until all those deadbeat assholes who made fun of me in school learn about this.*

I stayed in the military for an eventful six and a half years with missions in trouble-torn countries as far-flung as Africa and the Far East that are best not discussed. Like many veterans who have served their country, there are missions I *prefer* not to talk about and there are missions I can't talk about. There are also missions I'd prefer to forget.

When it came time to leave the army, I had the option to take a reserve commission, but almost all the officers whose advice I sought said that if they were in my shoes with my skills, it would make financial sense to focus on a career in civilian life. That turned out to be true.

While stationed at MacDill, I'd worked with a lot of scientists and executives from the major defense contractors. Thanks to those contacts, I was lucky to be offered jobs with both IBM and Honeywell. First, I flew up to New York to check out the IBM operation at Poughkeepsie. I took one look at all the people quietly slogging away in their little cubicles and saw that it was not for me. In fact, it would have been the death of me because I needed to interact with people.

Honeywell's aerospace division in Clearwater, right across the bay from MacDill, had a more laid-back atmosphere, which was definitely more my style, so I accepted their offer and went to work there.

The first task they gave me involved the experimental X-15, a hypersonic rocket-powered aircraft operated jointly by the United States Air Force and the National Aeronautics and Space Administration (NASA). It was a remarkable plane that set altitude and speed records.

Carried aloft and drop-launched from under the wing of a B-52 mother ship, the X-15 would ignite and soar to 100,000 feet, sometimes exceeding speeds of four thousand miles an hour. The X-15 didn't have any wheels, so we had to plan where it could touch down on its skids—places like salt flats or desert sand. And to choose a suitable landing site, we also had to calculate how long the plane had been in flight and how far it had traveled. It was a really exciting project.

My first calculations were not too clever. I plotted the plane flying in a straight line and failed to take into account the curvature of Earth, a vital piece of information when you think about planes flying at the edge of outer space. Fortunately, one of my colleagues, a smart girl who'd been to the Sorbonne in Paris, pointed out my error to me. She saved my ass, even if she did delight in one-upping me, using an apple to represent the curve of Earth as she demonstrated how I'd gone wrong.

Honeywell was quite an experience, but after a couple of years, I decided to move to Orlando to work for the giant NCR Corporation.

One of my biggest successes there was securing the Red Lobster restaurant chain as a client after working out a deal with cofounder Bill Darden, an astute businessman who started the first seafood chain in America and headquartered it in Orlando.

I sold Bill some incredible software that analyzed labor costs versus revenue on a real time basis and calculated the exact cost of every item on the menu, ingredient by ingredient. It allowed them to assess server productivity and table turnover—meaningful calculations for the company's bottom line. The only problem was that Bill didn't want to sign a contract.

"You got the business," he told me. "It's yours."

That wasn't going to cut it with NCR.

"I need a signed contract. NCR doesn't do handshake deals," I said.

"Well, I guess they don't want my business," Bill replied.

It was one hell of a dilemma. How could I get him to sign a contract? I came up with the idea of having the local newspaper, the *Orlando Sun Sentinel*, write a feature article and photograph him signing the contract—my contract—during the interview. Bill was all dressed up, looking good and proud as a peacock, and he dutifully signed the contract as the photographer snapped dozens of photos. I got out of there really fast, contract in hand.

General Mills later made Bill an offer he couldn't refuse to buy Red Lobster and also hired him as an executive. Today it has more than seven hundred locations worldwide.

It wasn't too long, though, before I decided I'd had enough of working for other people. I needed to be in charge of my own destiny. It was time to strike out on my own.

Chapter 4

The Million Dollar Man

It wasn't a David versus Goliath battle. It was David versus half a dozen Goliaths.

I've never feared anything and I've never been shy of a challenge. I've always believed in myself and pushed the envelope, knowing that God would open doors for me that I couldn't open myself. I've always reached for the stars, so I didn't hesitate when I learned that NASA was seeking bids to design the launch processing system for the Space Shuttle, the first spacecraft that would not only circle the planet but also be reusable.

I knew it was something I could do. I was sure I could create a breakthrough software program for them. But how could I get my foot in the door? I was a little pissant thing, and I'd be up against my former employer, Honeywell, as well as other multibillion-dollar aerospace firms like GE, IBM, Lockheed, Martin Marietta, and Northrop Grumman.

The first thing I did was recruit the help of my local congressman, Lou Frey. Luckily, he had the inside track because he served on NASA's science and technology committee. I explained my keen interest in the NASA project and said that I was concerned I'd be dismissed out of hand because I was small-time and had no prior experience working with the space agency. Lou was great. He arranged a meeting for me in Washington, DC, with NASA Administrator Dr James Fletcher, and he even accompanied me.

I frankly explained my situation. "I've been in this business long enough to know there's a big difference in how someone from a billion-dollar company is perceived and treated compared with someone from a million-dollar company. Will I get taken seriously?"

Dr. Fletcher said not to worry, they wanted everyone to participate.

That sounded like typical Washington political-speak BS to me. I pushed him. "Will you give that instruction to the evaluation committee down at the Kennedy Space Center?"

"No problem," he said.

Right there and then he called the committee director, Bill Bailey, and told him to give full consideration to my bid. (And yes, that really was his name.) I was in. It was all about perception. Bill Bailey was given the impression that I had the right connections and the right credentials. And he had to listen to what his boss said.

The bidders met with NASA personnel at the space center numerous times to go over project needs, and everyone thought it was funny as hell that I was there. I wasn't part of their club. I was the outsider, the foolish little guy with the southern accent from some no-name place in the wilds of Tennessee who didn't seem to grasp that he didn't have a cat in hell's chance of getting the business. It wasn't a David versus Goliath battle. It was David versus half a dozen Goliaths. It was preposterous to think I could procure this billion-dollar project. Wasn't it?

The other bidders showed their amusement about my presence in all kinds of ways. At the end of a morning meeting, the project leader might say, "We're going to take a break and we'll be back at one o'clock. Randy, just so you know, that's when the big hand is on the twelve and the little hand is on the one."

It was said in a good-natured manner, and everyone—including me—was in on the joke. I shouldn't be there. How could I be as smart

48

as the guys from the big-name aerospace giants who'd worked with NASA for years? They weren't taking me seriously. I was no competition. That's when I knew I had them, and I was going to get the last laugh.

I asked question after question, thousands of questions. I had to dig deep to figure out what I could bring to the table that the others couldn't.

One thing puzzled me. Like millions of people around the world, I'd watched the televised launches of the Apollo missions, most notably the epic landing of men on the moon. In the control room, rows and rows of men (and it was all men back then) sat in front of computer screens. They always seemed to be picking up a phone, nodding seriously, and scribbling notes. I wanted to know what kind of questions they asked and what kind of information they were fed. It turned out that these exchanges had to do with things like essential data about fuel levels, temperature readings, and valve pressures.

It was the most incredible nail-biting journey in the history of mankind, a 240,000-mile voyage to the moon, a mission that pushed the bounds of known technology. And in its vital control center, they had to resort to communication by telephone and note taking with pen and paper. What a waste of time. Seconds were critical when astronauts' lives and a billion-dollar space mission were on the line, and especially when that information could already be inaccurate by the time it was processed. My solution was to computerize the input of that data and automatically generate an interrupt on the computer screen if something was out of range.

They wanted to know how I suggested doing that, and I told them I was glad they'd asked.

I'd forged a relationship with a Florida-based company, Modular Computer Systems (MODCOMP). They had a very powerful computer that was interrupt driven instead of being reliant on human decision-making input.

MODCOMP's president, Ken Harple, agreed to provide their computer hardware and participate with the software engineering if I snagged the NASA account. It was a no-brainer for him. After all, it was potentially worth a billion dollars to them, and they had nothing to lose. Ken asked me what I thought my chances were.

"That business is mine," I told him confidently.

I was serious. I truly believed I could pull it off, although I didn't know that Ken shared my confidence.

As part of my business strategy, I persuaded the NASA guys to attend a meeting 170 miles down the coast at the MODCOMP office in Fort Lauderdale. For a lunch presentation, I set up a room with a bank of computers that had their guts exposed, arrayed along the walls. No matter where they sat, the NASA folks would be staring at an impressive display of computing power. It was pretty cool—quite a show. Against that backdrop, I explained my proposal to develop an interrupt system, knowing that neither Honeywell nor any of the other big boys, even with their huge teams of experts, could do that. And I wanted the NASA guys to appreciate the ruggedness of the computer system because I knew it would need to work for years.

I used the post office in my hometown of Middleton, Tennessee, to illustrate the concept. I explained that the post office had small individual mailboxes. You had a key to unlock your box, and you put mail in and took mail out. I could do something similar with the computer but on a much grander scale because of its huge memory array. I could put messages in and take messages out. I could control what went in, what came out, and who had access, based on their security level. I could also prioritize how quickly messages were transmitted. That's how I made a believer out of them. Nobody else could deliver an interrupt-driven program. The NASA folks were impressed and encouraged me to move forward. The concept for the Space Shuttle launch processing system was partly inspired by the little post office in Middleton, Tennessee.

I busted my ass. I worked day and night putting it all together. It damn near drove me crazy. I was so exhausted, I almost had a breakdown.

Two years after making the first proposal, the day arrived when NASA would announce who'd been awarded the contract. It was a tense, high-stakes event. Everyone had so much invested in the decision, and no one had more than me. I wasn't a tech giant with thousands of employees and hundreds of major accounts. I had everything riding on the outcome.

All the bidders sat nervously in a conference room at the Kennedy Space Center waiting for the announcement. It was kind of like the Oscars, awaiting the declaration, "And the winner is . . ." The project manager got up, and after a pause for dramatic effect, he announced that the contract went to MODCOMP and Randy Ray.

The big guys couldn't believe it. They were aghast. Dumbfounded. Shell-shocked. Someone exclaimed, "You've got to be kidding me!" I could barely keep myself from whooping and hollering.

On my way out, I said to the competition, "You boys be nice to me 'cause I might give you some business."

I did. I later handed IBM a ten million-dollar contract.

I got out of that room and the Kennedy Space Center as fast as I could. My feet didn't touch the ground. It was almost a billion-dollar account. The first phase was $250 million, and I knew my commission check would be six million dollars. I was thirty-two years old. I'd beat my goal of becoming a millionaire by the age of thirty-five—and then some. I'd accomplished it three years ahead of target, and I'd made five million more than my dream. I could buy all the food, clothes, cars, and homes that were on my childhood goal sheet. Eventually, the total commission payout from the deal was eighteen million dollars. I'd arrived. It was a lot more than I could have made laboring on the farm, the occupation my teachers had in mind for me.

Best of all, I'm proud to say that the software I created for NASA in conjunction with an incredible team of guys at MODCOMP never had to be changed. It performed flawlessly for thirty years, running all 135 Space Shuttle missions, and it connected with more than five hundred computers around the world, right through the final flight in 2011.

On a personal level, there was one strange incident during the NASA job. My project manager was a Canadian Jewish guy, David Josephs, whose wife, Raisel, invited me for a good home-cooked meal because I was always on the road. After she prepared and served a lovely dinner, the three of us sat at the table and chit-chatted about one thing or another.

The subject got around to my upbringing and my parents, and I said, "I really wish my mom had lived long enough to see how I turned out."

"She knows all about it," Raisel said. "She's very happy the way you turned out."

I couldn't fathom how she could possibly know that. My mom had been dead for years. She was only forty-eight, and I was still in high school when she passed away.

"She's standing right beside you," Raisel added.

And then she described my mom to a tee, even down to a little mole on her face. She said my dad was standing beside my mom, and she accurately described him as well.

"Would you like to talk to them?"

"Hell, no," I said.

I'd always been taught that stuff like that—communicating with the dead—was kind of like witchcraft and to steer clear of it. I freaked out. I couldn't handle it and fled from their home. I wish I'd said yes.

My work for NASA earned me a VIP pass for any of the Space Shuttle launches. When they first rolled out the shuttle at Rockwell's primary assembly factory in Palmdale, California, I mingled with heads of state, astronauts, and other dignitaries. I was so close to legendary broadcaster Walter Cronkite, I could put my hand on his shoulder. As I sat there, marveling at it all, I thought about the folks in Middleton who had seen me as nothing and no one. Instead of being just another sharecropper, I was rubbing elbows with the likes of Walter Cronkite because I had played a part in something important. I'd beaten the odds. It felt like a major victory.

The six million-dollar commission check went to my head. It was like winning the lottery. It was party time—time to celebrate after years of toil putting the NASA deal together. I went a little crazy. I'd never earned anything remotely like that kind of money. It was a far cry from the day I'd left home fifteen years earlier with less than two dollars to my name. I'd never had any kind of financial management advice, and I blew through money like a big shot, acquiring more "friends" than I'd ever known. I even flew groups of people to Spain, wining and dining them.

After six months of whooping it up, it hit me that blowing through a lot of money was a dumbass thing to do. Another of my dad's old sayings dawned on me: "You'll have two kinds of friends in life. You'll have fair-weather friends who are there when things are going well. But the true friends, those that would die for you, are your thumb buddies. You'll be lucky if you have two of them."

I needed thumb buddies, but I'd accumulated a gang of freeloaders who would be gone in an instant if the weather turned sour. There was a lot of truth to my dad's saying, and it brought me to my senses. I knew I had to stop. Fortunately, I hadn't squandered all the money, just enough to be a wakeup call. And I did put some of it to good use, paying off my family's homes and buying cars for those who didn't have them.

But it was time to get back to work. Developing software solutions was in my blood. I loved doing it, and I couldn't imagine doing anything else. So I started a company I called Daxko, designing software for the criminal justice system. We installed software for Florida sheriff's offices in Seminole, Hillsborough, Polk, and Orange counties, as well as the Oklahoma state court system and many other places.

One of the first software programs I created for the court system was designed to handle jury selection in the infamous case of Ted Bundy, the notorious serial killer and rapist who eventually confessed to the murder of thirty or more young women and girls in the 1970s. It was a complex, high-profile case, and other companies had failed to design a program that could sift through a wide range of criteria to make sure there was nothing questionable in the backgrounds of potential jurors. I got immense satisfaction from developing a program that others couldn't and that performed exactly as required.

While running Daxko, I spent more than a year in Ireland, courtesy of the Irish Development Authority's attractive tax incentives and business development program. Not only did the criminal justice system in Ireland buy our software programs, but at about the same time, I pulled off my biggest deal, a two million-dollar contract providing computers to the British Aircraft Corporation.

It was a wonderful time in my life. I loved Ireland and its charming people. But there were business storm clouds back in the States that needed to be resolved, so I returned home and sold Daxko to a company in Canada called Cavendish Investing Limited. It was time for another chapter in my life.

Chapter 5

The Love of My Life

Wendy and I have the perfect partnership in so many ways.

I like to tell people that when I first met Wendy, I heard the heavenly choir singing. But it wasn't quite like that. Far from it.

I was running the sales department for a company in Orlando called US Medical Systems that helped doctors computerize their offices. Computers were beginning to take over from outmoded paper and pegboard systems. It was a business sector with huge growth potential.

The moment I walked into my office one morning, the receptionist said, "This lady is really furious with you. She says you don't call her back, so you must not need business."

The lady was Wendy. She was installing a computer system at her husband's medical office. I didn't have any messages from her, and I definitely would not have failed to return a sales inquiry. I quickly called the number and got the same earful of criticism: You can't need business. You don't return your calls. I've called several times. No one has gotten back to me.

"Ma'am, I have no record of you calling," I told her.

That's when I discovered she'd phoned our sales guy in Tampa. His lack of follow-up explained why he wasn't producing any sales—and why I fired him soon afterward.

Once we got that squared away, I invited Wendy to come into the office for a demonstration of our software and asked what day she would like to come in.

Wendy insisted I go to her house because she said she couldn't leave, and she wanted me there the same day. Although that seemed a bit odd, I didn't want to antagonize her more, so I obliged. The reason she couldn't leave was immediately obvious when I arrived on her doorstep later that day. Clinging to her leg and peering up at me as she opened the front door was an adorable little girl with pigtails, her two-year-old daughter, who was covered in chicken pox.

The computer demo became an interrogation. She threw question after question at me. Heck, I'd sold hundreds of millions of dollars of equipment to NASA without being subjected to such a barrage of questions. This lady knew what she wanted, and she was not exactly pleased with my presentation.

Basically, I didn't know the answers to some of her questions.

"Your questions are more extensive than I'd expected," I said. "Let me schedule someone else to help you out."

I arranged for a really smart kid who worked for me to go back and give her another demo. Luckily, he did a great job, and she wound up buying the system. (Otherwise, we might not be together today.)

But Wendy was not an easy customer. She had sky-high standards and demanded nothing but the best. I sent trainers to her office, and after a few hours she sent them back because she said they didn't know what they were doing. She also discovered that the software couldn't perform as advertised. I hadn't known that, but it didn't make her any happier that I didn't. And without the benefit of our training, she completely mastered the software, which didn't happen with most customers.

Wendy had her own consultancy business, and over time, it

became obvious that she really knew her stuff. So I recruited her to work with me. She wrote a lesson plan to train the trainers and collaborated with me on other projects. For about three years, my principle role was sales while Wendy took care of the training.

It got to the point where we were spending an awful lot of time together. I was impressed with her business acumen, and we realized that we made a great team. During that time, I was getting unhappier and unhappier with my role at US Medical Systems.

"I've had enough," I said to Wendy one day. "I've got to leave what I'm doing. I can't keep doing this. Let's set up a business together and do our own thing."

We took the operation she'd been running as an individual and formed our own company, Automated Medical Systems Consultants (AMSC). Wendy found Medical Manager, an innovative software program developed by a guy named Mickey Singer who owned Personalized Programming Inc. He was quite a character. He'd founded a spiritual-based community called the Temple of the Universe, which was a yoga and meditation center open to people regardless of their religious beliefs. The stated goal was for them to acquire inner peace

Mickey wanted to demo the software, so we met him at his compound on six hundred acres of land at Alachua, just outside Gainesville, Florida. We were there until one in the morning and had to drive home in pouring rain, but we were sold. Mickey's program beat the heck out of what I was selling at US Medical Systems and made it a lot easier for physicians to manage their billing and patient records.

That program became the number one software in the US, and even today, it is widely used in doctors' offices across the country. In our first year, we became the top dealer in the Southeast in both sales and service for Systems Plus, the marketing arm that sold the software. In our second year and for the next seven years, we were the number one dealer in the entire country. We were doing extremely well.

Then Mickey decided to take Personalized Programming public, and we didn't know what the future might have in store for dealerships. Coincidentally, an opportunity came along to sell our business to a Tulsa-based outfit, CIS Technologies. But when they first approached us with a proposal, Wendy was reluctant to sell the company.

"It's my baby," she said.

"We can have more babies," I replied.

CIS Technologies didn't want the hardware, just the software, so in 1994, we sold that side of the business to them for five million dollars. We turned the hardware division into a new entity, Alpha Computer Services (ACS), which installed and maintained computers and printers.

Our relationship with Personalized Programming was so good that when they went public, they gave each of us five thousand shares of family and friends stock that was selling for about nine dollars a share. Then the stock took off. When it hit eighteen dollars a share, I determined it was time to cash in and told Wendy that we needed to sell.

I sold my shares and was happy. It was a nice profit by anyone's standards. But Wendy was smarter and held on to her stock until the price hit thirty-nine dollars a share. I should have listened to her, and she's never let me live that down.

Our working relationship couldn't have been better. Although we were both analytical types, I was outgoing and sales-oriented while Wendy was a bit shy and phenomenal on the operational side of the business. We were so compatible and working so hard, we seemed to spend all our time together. It was probably inevitable that the relationship evolved into a romantic one. Wendy's husband had left her, and my marriage had been over for a long time.

My nephew and a few other people ran the day-to-day operation for us while we built a house and enjoyed some vacation time before returning to work full-time. Retirement was definitely not in the cards for us. Besides, Wendy's kids, who were teenagers, told her that she was too young to retire. But she jokingly admits that they probably just didn't want her around the house.

Alpha Computer Services began to grow like crazy. Our growth was so sensational, we were ranked 184 in the *Inc. 500* list of America's fastest-growing, privately held companies.

The *Inc.* magazine report generated a ton of interest. All kinds of companies interested in acquiring such a successful business beat a path to our door. The timing for us was perfect. We could see that the trend in the marketplace was away from minicomputers and into PCs. Prices were coming down. Anyway, we'd had enough of changing hard drives and calculated that the demand for computer maintenance was bound to decline. It was the same for printers, which were becoming disposable commodities. When they broke, people just threw them away and bought new ones. It was the ideal time to move on, and we were delighted to sell Alpha Computer Services for twenty-four million dollars.

While we owned that company, we had a separate business called MarketQ that hosted computers for network marketing and direct sales companies. Mostly, we worked with startups that did not have the financial resources or expertise to set up their own in-house operation.

We'd already had some experience with the network marketing industry. When we had the medical services company, Amway was a popular business opportunity for doctors, and we were approached all the time. It seemed like every week a doctor would ask us what we were doing Thursday night, and we knew that was going to lead to an invitation to one of the infamous Amway recruiting meetings. We eventually signed up as Amway distributors, primarily to keep doctors from bothering us. It was easier just to say, "We're already distributors."

We did give it something of a shot, or at least I did. Because Wendy was so shy, I was the one who did most of the talking and training. I went to people's homes to do the presentations. If someone who became a distributor didn't do well in spite of my best efforts, I felt bad for them, even if they hadn't tried all that hard. Wendy liked to point out that even though it wasn't my responsibility, I gave those folks their money back, money they had paid to Amway. Not a good business model.

One day she said to me, "Randy, this is a problem. We're going to go broke if you keep doing that." In other words, stop right now.

With our MarketQ company, Wendy developed part of the business that became hugely successful—creating sophisticated multilevel compensation plans and fixing other people's attempt to create plans, something few people in the country had the expertise to do. Wendy held BA degrees in sociology and mathematics from the University of Pennsylvania and a master's degree in educational psychology, statistics, and measurement from Temple University. Besides that, she taught mathematics for eight years. All in all, you couldn't ask for a more perfect combination of credentials to write viable compensation plans that not only greatly motivated and rewarded distributors for their efforts but also ensured that the payout was within a company's budget.

On top of that, she had great entrepreneurial instincts. At the age of eight, this woman opened a "summer camp" in her parents' back patio, charging neighborhood kids to take part in arts and crafts projects and play lawn games.

Our services expanded. We began to provide customer support, something with which we were familiar from our medical companies. We handled order entry, banking, packing, and shipping. Eventually, we became the entire back-office operation for fifteen direct sales and network marketing companies, each having its own unique requirements. Some of them still exist today and are doing extremely well.

We were the entire infrastructure for a lot of startups, doing everything for them. This was before the existence of the internet. People would enroll in a company and we'd get the forms sent to us by fax. Then we entered the information and made bank deposits of payments. They couldn't take credit cards back then, so we handled cash, checks, and certified checks. There was a lot of manual processing until it became possible to do everything online. It gave us the kind of experience in the industry that very few company owners can claim to have had.

We never turned away business. If someone asked us if we could do something, we always said, "Yes, we can do that." We became the can-do company. That also meant that Wendy and I continued to spend an incredible amount of time together—at work and at home— something we absolutely loved.

Wendy and I have the perfect partnership in so many ways. We don't fight. That's probably because I learned early on to say, "Yes, ma'am." (Okay, I'm joking.) What is true is that we've been married thirty-five years, and she lights my fire every day. I love her more with every passing year. The beauty of our relationship is that we can both look at something, be in full agreement, and then go full bore with blood, sweat, and tears to make it happen.

What drives Wendy is her desire to be the best and provide service of excellence to everyone. I can wake up at 2:30 in the morning and hear click, click, click because she's looking something up on her cell phone or she's writing an email.

"Why aren't you sleeping?" I ask her. "You can do that in the morning." But she never stops.

For ten years at MarketQ, we developed a reputation for launching businesses. Then we came across a unique product that spurred us to launch our own network marketing company in November 2005, Fuel Freedom International (FFI). The product was a fuel additive that you put in the gas tank of your vehicle to improve fuel efficiency, deliver more miles per gallon, and reduce the emission of pollutants. The additive, a pill that we called MPG-Cap, was a completely organic engine conditioner that worked by creating a micro-thin coating on the combustion chamber.

The business grew quickly. For our first-year anniversary, we hosted more than eighteen hundred distributors from around the world at a convention in Orlando. At another convention, Wendy and I had some fun during the opening event at Disney's Coronado Springs Resort. While Wendy was on stage making a welcome speech, a film was shown of me playing golf with Mickey Mouse. Pretending to be annoyed that I was goofing off and not at the event, she demanded to know what I thought I was doing, just as I sank a putt. Then the film cut to Mickey and me jumping in the golf cart and racing past familiar Disney locations. As Wendy got ever-more impatient, I drove the golf cart onto the stage, along with my famous passenger.

"Hi everyone," I announced. "It's all under control."

Within seventeen months, we were doing one hundred million dollars a year with distributors and customers as far afield as countries where they have really nasty fuel, like China and Russia. We built a network of more than eighty thousand distributors in 126 countries. We learned a lot in terms of what to do and what not to do when opening a business in a foreign country, but we ran into a major challenge. The dirtier the fuel, the better the product worked, but the fuel companies started using less sulfur in the gas, especially in the American market. The quality of gas improved so much that the need for MPG-Cap began to decline.

FFI gave us a wonderful foundation. Expanding internationally at such a rapid rate presented numerous challenges we'd never encountered before and which we learned how to overcome. Not everything we did was perfect. We made our share of mistakes. But the experience gave us knowledge that was to prove invaluable when we created the business that has eclipsed everything we'd done before and has transformed so many lives across the world: Jeunesse Global.

Chapter 6

The Birth of Jeunesse

I'd never been averse to taking risks. I'd always jumped hook, line, and sinker into anything I wanted to do.

Excruciating knee pain, bone on bone, took me to a doctor's office—and led to the creation of Jeunesse Global. Here's how it happened.

My right knee was shot to pieces. It was worn and torn. The damage probably started during my time in the US Army's Special Forces when I jumped out of planes and did other crazy stuff. The pain was so bad I could barely walk, and I had to do something about it. Otherwise, I'd end up in a wheelchair. Doctors recommended knee replacement surgery, but that didn't appeal to me. I really wanted to keep my original equipment, so to speak.

I checked all over the world for alternatives and found a controversial procedure in which stem cells from a person's bone marrow were injected into their knee to regenerate cartilage. It was not approved in the US, but a group of doctors in Singapore had successfully carried out the procedure. The science was sound and there were glowing testimonials from numerous people who had avoided the agony of knee replacement. I was all set to fly off to Singapore for a month to have the stem cell procedure.

Then a friend told us about a doctor in Beverly Hills, Dr. Nathan Newman, a renowned cosmetic surgeon, dermatologist, and pioneer in stem cell technology who had even performed operations at Cook County Hospital in Chicago to help regrow skin for children who had been badly burned.

We were impressed by his résumé. He went to the University of Southern California, got his medical degree at Albert Einstein College of Medicine in New York, completed his internship in internal medicine at UCLA-VA Medical Center in Los Angeles, and did his residency in dermatology at Chicago's Cook County Hospital. He obtained his fellowship through the American Academy of Cosmetic Surgery. His credentials were impeccable and he was highly recommended.

When we met with him at his Beverly Hills office, he explained his procedure. Instead of extracting stem cells from bone marrow, he'd take them from my adipose tissue (that's fat to me and you), spin it down, and extract the stem cells, which would then be injected into my knee. I was no longer the skinny kid who signed up for the army, and I could supply as much fat as they needed.

It was a big leap of faith because it was the first time the procedure would be carried out in the US, and it was subject to some restrictions. In particular, everything had to be done in the same operating room. The extracted stem cells could not be taken off the premises. But that had always been the story of my life. I'd never been averse to taking risks. I'd always jumped hook, line, and sinker into anything I wanted to do. So around Easter 2009, I went in for the procedure, which Dr. Newman arranged to have filmed because it was such a big deal. He decided to extract the fat from my waist. I offered fifty-five gallons of high-quality blubber, but unfortunately, he only needed 60 ccs.

With the cameras rolling, I lay there on a cold table in a freezing cold room with nothing more than a small washcloth to cover my essentials, even though I told them a beach towel was more appropriate.

68

Patiently waiting in the reception area, Wendy was intrigued by some small vials she spotted in a display cabinet. The receptionist told her it was a proprietary serum developed by Dr. Newman that dramatically got rid of the appearance of fine lines and wrinkles without the need for scalpels or lasers. That grabbed Wendy's attention, and when they showed her stunning before and after photos, she was completely sold and told them she needed to try it.

When we returned to Florida, Wendy was armed with a bottle of the serum and I had a "regenerated" knee that was hopefully going to last a while.

The serum delivered remarkable results. Within a couple of weeks, you could see the difference, particularly around the eyes, but also on Wendy's entire face. It was so noticeable, people kept asking what she'd done. Did I get to try the serum even though my wrinkly face really needed it? Nope. Wendy kept it all for herself. Obviously, it was too good to share.

Then she said to me, "Randy, this is something that would really sell."

"You're right." I agreed not because I knew better than to disagree but because she was right. "This could be big, really big. It could go worldwide."

The product had all of the right elements for a network marketing company. It was unique: the world's only skin care facial serum based on stem cell technology. The results were demonstrable and striking. And it was highly consumable. People would buy the product again and again. The potential for reorders was immense.

We set up another meeting with Dr. Newman, not to talk about my knee (which was doing great) but specifically about his serum.

"How many of these do you sell a month?" I asked.

"About forty, just to my patients."

Forty? Four-zero? Good grief, I thought. "How would you like to sell forty thousand?"

Dr. Newman laughed. "I'd love to, but I don't have a clue how to do that."

"We do," we said with one voice. "Share your formula with us and we'll make it happen."

That's what we did. We sold forty thousand bottles the first month. Since then, we've sold more than nine million. I'm sure Dr. Newman never anticipated that kind of volume.

After the Beverly Hills meeting with Dr. Newman, we went back to Florida and went to work. We sat around our conference room for a brainstorming session with half a dozen of our top people including Wendy's son Scott, Lucy West, who is still with us today as executive director of global field development, and Brian Trustman, who's now our senior director of marketing operations. What was the core message of this new company we were going to create? What would it all be about? Our initial concept was to focus on youth-enhancing products. To us, the commonly used term "antiaging" sounded somewhat negative, whereas "youth-enhancing" was positive.

What should we call this new entity? Wendy was adamant that we shouldn't invent some meaningless word that people have trouble pronouncing and remembering, never mind spelling. For some odd reason, that's what many direct sales companies did. We wanted a name that meant something, one that would epitomize the nature of the business. Between us, we came up with dozens of names, but they had either already been taken or didn't excite us. Then it hit us: Jeunesse, the French word for youth or youthfulness. It had the perfect ring to it. Not only did it sound exotic, it also made you think of quality and classiness. The instant the word was spoken, there was consensus that we'd found our identity. It was one of those classic eureka moments.

Then we had to create a product name that would be compatible with Jeunesse and also capture the essence of the skin care serum. Again, we bounced dozens and dozens of names off each other. We weren't short of ideas, that's for sure. The answer: Luminesce™. Like Jeunesse, it sounded right, and it was bang on target in terms of its meaning. Look up the word "luminescent" in the thesaurus and you'll discover synonyms like "glowing," "radiant," "shining," and "bright." Bingo. Luminesce—an outstanding name for a skin care product. Both names were conjured up in one creative brainstorming session, which was quite an accomplishment.

While Dr. Newman's original serum was superb, we had to make it suitable for the mass market and compliant with regulations for ingredients and labeling that differed country by country. Further research enabled us to improve the product's absorption into the skin and formulate it using natural preservatives, a major selling point for many consumers. Of course, we kept the key active component from fat cells, the stem cell derivative named Human Adipose Stromal Cell Conditioned Media Extract. It was such a mouthful, we branded it APT-200!

Basically, what happens is that the stromal cells, extracted from human fat, are grown into thousands of new cells in the lab. The "conditioned media extract" is simply the solution (sugars, amino acids, etc.) in which the cells are grown. Subsequently, we were able to develop and market a plant-based version that worked exactly the same way and was preferred in many countries.

From long experience, we knew it wasn't wise to launch as a one-product company, and we decided the ideal strategy was to open our doors with two youth-enhancing products: one that worked from the inside out and one that worked from the outside in. The outside in product was Luminesce.

Scott, who is now the company's chief visionary officer, took the lead developing the inside-out product. Working with our manufacturer, he investigated a polyphenol called resveratrol which is found in red wine and the skin of red grapes. Newly published research showed it had potential benefits for the heart and for longevity. Because you couldn't drink enough red wine to get enough resveratrol to have a health impact, some other companies that had recognized its potential sold it in pills or capsules. There was no way we were going to have a me-too product. That wasn't our style. We came up with a novel approach: Serve the resveratrol and a blend of other botanical antioxidants in a tasty bioavailable gel. It provided a much better experience than popping a pill. We called it Reserve™. Luminesce and Reserve made the perfect opening double act.

Two key motives lay behind this venture for Wendy and me: helping adults and helping children. We had been blessed with financial good fortune from building and selling businesses, and we felt it was time to give back. Helping adults included providing an exciting income opportunity. The economy was in bad shape. A lot of people had lost their jobs. One of our goals was to give people a way to carve their own destiny by setting and achieving their own goals. And, as far as children were concerned, my own impoverished childhood stimulated a tender spot for kids born in similar or worse circumstances. So Wendy and I decided to become advocates for disadvantaged children around the world to improve their education and their health. We were determined to make it big: The more successful the business became, the more adults and kids we could help.

We had the products and we had the company name. We had the core corporate team, people who already worked with us at Fuel Freedom International, and we had the same offices in Altamonte

Springs, Florida, less than thirty miles from Disney World. All of that was in place.

Another essential element for a winning network marketing business was the compensation plan, one of Wendy's areas of expertise. She took the comp plan she'd created for Fuel Freedom International and enhanced it, making it more attractive for distributors to climb to higher ranks, giving them the opportunity to earn greater income. She added bonus pools to make it even more rewarding. It was a binary plan but with matching bonuses through seven levels. That plan has been copied over and over, which tells you how good it is.

The final element we needed to make the company successful was a team of passionate, hardworking distributors. The first person we thought of was Kim Hui, a former distributor with FFI who was originally from Hong Kong. We felt the business was perfect for her, so we visited her in Southern California and explained our concept and products to her over lunch. Kim's initial response was not too positive. She didn't get it until she went home and discussed it with her husband, a doctor. He got very excited. He told her that stem cells were the future of medicine, that it was a wonderful idea, and that she already knew Randy and Wendy could make things happen. His enthusiasm convinced her.

Kim started building her network at her kitchen table with four people who all lived in the LA area: Tina Hu from Greater China, Samson Li from Hong Kong, Robert Nhan from Vietnam, and Winny Sutandyo from Indonesia. We called them The Big Five. They're all still part of our Jeunesse family and have become financially secure for life. We worked hard and fast. From the time I had my stem cell procedure to launch was less than five months.

The official unveiling of Jeunesse Global was September 9, 2009 at 9:00 p.m. That's 9-9-9-9. In Chinese, the number nine sounds like "forever lasting." In other words, it represents longevity. Perfect! At 9:00 p.m., we went live with a global conference call and stared at the computer screens as the first surge of registrations poured in. Jeunesse Global was officially in business with two products, a website, and a brochure. And that was it.

A few weeks earlier, no more than a hundred people were brought by The Big Five to a prelaunch meeting at the Hilton Hotel in San Gabriel, California, ten miles east of downtown Los Angeles, to hear us explain our vision. All a bit different from today when twenty thousand distributors sometimes fill stadiums for events. And we could have even bigger crowds if locations were available to accommodate everyone who'd like to attend.

Getting prepared for the prelaunch was nail-biting down to the wire as we waited to get final samples of the Reserve product manufactured and delivered to the hotel. Thankfully, the samples arrived the morning of the meeting, although not in the finished packaging. Instead, the Reserve gel was supplied in glass bottles with stoppers and rubber bands tied around the top. We scrambled to get paper cups from a nearby store so we could serve the samples.

And with our not particularly impressive looking samples, we had the nerve to stand there and announce that we were going to be the next billion-dollar network marketing company. It didn't matter. The potential distributors loved the taste of Reserve and the feel of Luminesce. They were blown away by the health benefits of the products and the financial benefits possible through the compensation plan. The prelaunch couldn't have gone any better. You could tell they were going to get out there and make things happen.

One lady made a point of putting Luminesce on just one hand so she could compare it with the other hand. To this day, she's only used

Luminesce on one hand, and the difference is striking. She's like a walking billboard.

It's also remarkable that these two products, Luminesce and Reserve, continue to be our bestsellers. Reserve is number one by far, having sold more than a billion packets. But most of all, it's astonishing to think that five people brought a small group to a meeting in a nondescript California hotel and that has mushroomed to 675,000 active distributors across the globe.

Though it was unusual for a network marketing company, our goal from day one was to go global. Instead of establishing roots in the US market and then expanding overseas, we turned the conventional approach on its head. We didn't call the company Jeunesse Global because it sounded like a big deal or because we wanted to pose as a big international outfit. We knew we were going to become a big international outfit, so we needed a name that fit.

We set out to expand into as many countries as we could as quickly as we could with a target of doing one million dollars in business a month in each country.

A major positive influence was the fact that our initial group of American-based distributors were experienced network marketers who were all Asian and had family, friends, acquaintances, and many other contacts back in their home countries.

That was a key reason we focused on Asian countries rather than the US, but it wasn't the only reason. We'd witnessed many American companies in the network marketing industry enjoy tremendous rapid growth only to hit a plateau and then spectacularly crash and burn. Unfortunately, many distributors in the US tend to jump from company to company when something seemingly more exciting comes along—the grass is greener syndrome.

The other sound reason for focusing globally was that Americans often looked to see what was wrong with an opportunity. It wasn't unusual to hear someone say, "I got into this network marketing deal and wasted three hundred dollars trying to sell their products. It never worked for me."

Of course, network marketing doesn't work for a person who doesn't work for it. Distributors in other countries, especially in Asia, are much more inclined to just go for it. They want to know the basics: How they make money. How much money they can make. What's good about the products. Why the products work. How many people can use them. Then they roll up their sleeves and get to work.

Our strategy was to establish legal business entities in each country, register the products, obtain licenses, join direct selling associations, recruit top-class management teams, and do everything open and above board—with an eye on the long haul. Part of the rationale for opening in multiple countries was that if one country suffered a downturn in sales, for whatever reason, it would be cushioned by sales in other countries. That's the way it has worked out. While there are countries that generate fifty million dollars or sixty million dollars a month in sales and others that do five million or ten million, it accumulates to over one billion dollars a year. If sales decline in one country, chances are that they go up in another country. Beyond that, there's always room for growth.

Our first office outside the States opened in Taiwan, followed by Hong Kong and Indonesia. It was based on wherever the sales volume was greatest, and we still follow that principle today. You must have great leadership in the field in a country and sales. Otherwise, there's no point opening an office there. We need to first see that there's a real grassroots demand.

We were on our way. We were workhorses, and we had a group of top leaders in the field who were workhorses. Together we could make it happen. Wendy and I had enjoyed success with previous businesses, for sure. Specifically, we'd had great experience at every level with network marketing: as distributors, running the back-office operations for other companies, and then launching our own global enterprise. We'd seen the good, the bad, and the really ugly. But I knew from the moment Wendy raved about Dr. Newman's skin care product that we'd found the vehicle for a massive international business.

As a kid I'd dreamed big and had no doubt I would be hugely successful. I didn't know then exactly how I was going to do it. But when we created Jeunesse, that was the vehicle for great success. As I said earlier, at the age of fourteen, one of my goals in life was to travel the world and meet other people. Not only was I on the verge of accomplishing that goal and building a legacy company to continue generation after generation, I was also on a path to helping tens of thousands of people make good supplemental income and even, in some cases, achieve financial security. And at the same time, lift children from the depths of poverty.

My mom in 1930, age 20.

With older brother JR, age 20, in his army uniform,
outside Aunt Tenny's house. I was 12.

Me at the age of 12.

SCHOOL DAYS 1953-54
MIDDLETON

My brother Winfred, age 9.

An artist's rendering of what my dad and I looked like when I was
twelve and he was in his early fifties.

With brothers Winfred (left) and JR (center) and sister Wanda.

My dad when he was about 75 years old.

Specialist E-5 Randy Ray receives football championship award
at the Presidio of San Francisco in 1963.

Wendy and me around 1985. Early days of AMSC.

Wendy, Winfred (right), and me, about 1988.

With my brothers Winfred (left) and JR (right.) Circa 2004.

With Jack Kracklauer, developer of Fuel Freedom International's
MPG-Cap. 2004.

Playing golf with Mickey Mouse during FFI's annual convention
in 2006 at Disney's Coronado Springs Resort.
Along with longest-serving employee Geri Dorman.

Rafting on the Nantahala in North Carolina. Wendy's daughter
Kymberly Lewis is front left and her friend Stephanie, front right.
July 3, 2008.

On a Mediterranean cruise with Fuel Freedom International, 2010.
Wendy is afraid that I might burst into song.

A visit to Russia to promote Fuel Freedom International.

Back to the beginning. With Dr. Nathan Newman, whose serum led to the founding of Jeunesse. At the Luxe Sunset Boulevard Hotel, Bel Air, Los Angeles, 2009.

On stage. Bangkok EXPO, August 2011.

We were thrilled to be witnesses at the wedding of Double Diamond
Director, Jason Chiang, and his wife Carin, in Taipei, Taiwan,
June 2012.

Saying hello to a cheetah. First Diamond Discovery Trip.
South Africa, 2013.

Cocktails at the Gondwana Private Game Reserve, South Africa,
during the Diamond Discovery Trip.

With Jason Chiang, wife Carin, and their daughter Jeunesse
during the 2014 Diamond Discovery Trip to the Greek Islands.

Arriving in Dao Lazui on the first Jeunesse Kids visit to a sponsored
community, December 2015.

January 2015. With Tina Hu.

Onstage kiss for the love of my life, November 2015.

Jeunesse Distributors proudly pose outside a classroom we built in Dao Lazui.

Applauding 11-year-old Li Meng's moving speech in the Dao Lazui classroom, December 2015.

Breaking ground in Dao Lazui.

Young Li Meng really bonded
with Wendy.

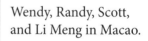

Wendy, Randy, Scott,
and Li Meng in Macao.

Digging for gold? Top leaders, including Ming Lee (left) and Tina Hu (right), give me a helping hand with the shovel.

Trying to hand out backpacks full of school supplies.

Celebrating with Jeunesse distributors who did the water walk, carrying 50-pound barrels on their backs. Irkaat, Kenya, July 2016.

Happy students at the Kisaruni Girls School, July 2016.

Training to be Maasai Warriors, July 2016.

We don't dress like this every day. At home in Florida, September 2016.

Soaking up the sun in Lahaina, Maui. Pacific'o restaurant, 2016.

Posing with Wendy and a group of Jeunesse Distributors at the Irkaat village in Kenya before planting seedlings for the community, 2016.

At the podium.

The little boy who latched on to me and wouldn't let go.

Love the headgear! Roaring Twenties dinner for Diamond Directors.
Orlando, Florida, circa 2016.

À *votre santé*. Dinner cruise on the River Seine in Paris in 2017.
From left to right, Estelle Norvell (Debbie's friend),
Debbie Kurley (niece), Scott, Isabel, Wendy, and me.

Hello from India. Group shot during the "Bringing Hope" stay at the WE Charity property in Araveli, July 2018.

Getting a helping hand from the children of Kalinjar, India, July 2018.

Look at those smiling faces. Local kids and Jeunesse distributors salute construction underway, July 2018.

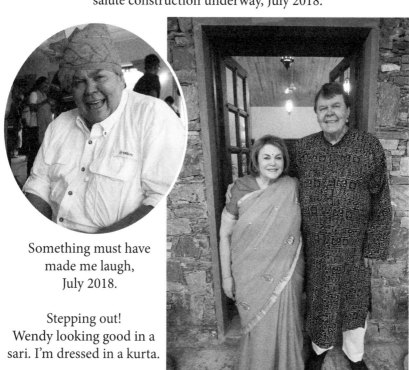

Something must have made me laugh, July 2018.

Stepping out! Wendy looking good in a sari. I'm dressed in a kurta.

Peek-a-boo! Having fun at the farewell dinner, India, 2018, in a hotel across from the Taj Mahal.

With Wendy, Scott, and Isabel, Emerald Experience Trip, Maui, 2018.

Making the founders' speech at the Jeunesse University event in Hong Kong, 2019.

Wendy must have said something funny. Discover Jeunesse event at the office in Lake Mary, 2019.

And the Oscar goes to… On stage at the Dolby Theatre, Hollywood, home of the Academy Awards for a Jeunesse LEAD event, January 2019.

Giving the founders' presentation at the Jeunesse Greater China NEXT EXPO 2019 in Macau.

Original Jeunesse building.

Jeunesse world headquarters, 2020.

Celebrating ten incredible years with the Jeunesse Family at the
Jeunesse EXPO 2019 NEXT event in Orlando, September 2019.

Chapter 7

The Jeunesse Journey

One Team. One Family. One Jeunesse.

W e took off like a rocket, and we've kept shooting for the stars. Since the company launched in 2009, Jeunesse has achieved and sustained extraordinary growth by any standard.

The numbers tell part of the story:

- We've hit more than one billion dollars in sales for five years in a row.

- We have more than 675,000 active distributors in more than 145 countries.

- We've notched up more than 720 awards from organizations such as Ernst & Young, the American Business Awards (the Stevies), and major industry publication *Direct Selling News*.

- We reached the position of number thirteen in the world on the *DSN Global 100* list.

We're very proud of our success, which we simply couldn't have accomplished without the support of a wonderful corporate team that has grown to nearly one thousand people. Some of our employees have worked with us for more than twenty years in various enterprises; others we hired because of their talent and extensive network marketing experience.

We strive to make Jeunesse a family environment and run the business with a servant's heart, which is probably why DSN rated us for four years as a "best place to work." We strive to live up to our company motto: One Team. One Family. One Jeunesse.

Of course, the business largely depends on our home-based distributors whose love for our products and magnificent efforts have brought us to where we now are. Great distributors make or break you. They're the lynchpin of the business. My philosophy is that the company should provide distributors with top-class products and a generous compensation plan, plus training and support, and then get out of their way.

In addition to our in-house team and distributors in the field, we have the backing and wisdom of a well-regarded scientific advisory board and product development group.

We need all of these partners to work synergistically together because Jeunesse Global is a 24/7 operation, a company that never sleeps. For instance, Asia, which is our biggest market, is awake and working when most people in the States have gone to bed.

It might seem strange to say, but from the beginning I knew we were destined to become a major player in the industry. What I didn't know was that we would achieve the annual sales milestone of one billion dollars faster than companies like Amazon, Amway, and Microsoft and have a greater first five years of business than Mary Kay had in its first twenty years. It is not surprising, therefore, that we're the youngest company in the network marketing industry to achieve billion-dollar status.

Let's go back to that first year. We hit the ground running, thanks to a seasoned, industry-knowledgeable staff, a core group of talented distributors, and the technological infrastructure to handle sales in numerous countries and pay commissions and bonuses, some of them weekly, through a complex multilevel structure. It was a launch sequence as dynamic and successful as my involvement in the first Space Shuttle mission twenty-eight years earlier.

Jeunesse Global is part of the direct selling industry, a $192 billion worldwide market involving 118 million representatives, and in the US, sales of $35 billion a year generated by 6 million distributors.

As a network marketing company, independent distributors register to sell our products and recruit others to sell our products. They earn profits not only on their own personal product sales but also on the sales made by members of their network. It's a business opportunity in which individuals are in business *for* themselves but not *by* themselves because they not only have the support of the company, they also have the support of other distributors in their network. Mostly, they work from home and invest as much time and effort as they want, setting their own schedule and choosing how and when to work.

A distributor's first connection with Jeunesse often happens when they fall in love with one or more of our products. It's a logical next step to become a distributor to purchase products at wholesale prices for personal use and sell them to friends and acquaintances if they want to earn extra pocket money. If they want to make enough to achieve a short-term goal—like buying a luxury item of some kind—that's fine too. It's not a difficult business. If you love a product, it's natural to want to tell others about it in just the same way you'd enthuse about a favorite movie or a wonderful new restaurant.

If a distributor desires a full-time career, that opportunity exists. Depending on their effort and skill set, they can make thousands of dollars—even tens of thousands—a year. And if they want to work exceptionally hard, they can generate income most people only dream about. But it's important to remember, no one earns money from re-cruiting, only from the sale of products.

Network marketing is a highly competitive industry, so when we launched, we had to be sure our compensation plan would be highly competitive and appeal to the goals of distributors: those who wanted to make a little money fast and those who had their eyes set on climbing the ranks to higher earnings.

We opened Jeunesse Global with a ten-year plan, not a ten-minute plan like some companies that elect to go into network marketing, an often-controversial industry that has been tarnished by unscrupulous get rich quick promoters.

Our core group of distributors rolled up their sleeves and passion-ately spread the word. From the US to Taiwan, Hong Kong, Indonesia, and beyond, product sales were extraordinary, generated by thousands of distributors who quickly joined our ranks.

Our first-year sales with just two products, the Luminesce Cellular Rejuvenation Serum and the Reserve gel, totaled thirty million dollars, an accomplishment few startups can claim. We more or less doubled sales year after year until we hit a billion dollars for the year in 2015, a significant milestone we've maintained for five years. It would be nice to keep doubling by the year, but that's not a realistic prospect once you reach that kind of sales volume.

Within the first two years, in response to distributor requests, we added two products to the Luminesce line, Luminesce Daily Moisturizing Complex and Luminesce Advanced Night Repair. And to handle the international business built by a network of distributors who had mushroomed to fifty thousand, we opened offices in twelve countries.

At our second annual expo, we added two nutritional supplements formulated by Nobel Prize nominee and board-certified plastic reconstructive surgeon Vincent C. Giampapa, MD. Both products, AM Essentials™, to help you "get up and go" in the morning, and PM Essentials™, a restorative nighttime formula, have different proprietary blends of more than seventy vitamins, minerals, and botanicals.

As we began to explore the development of more innovative, youth-enhancing products, we established a scientific advisory board. Dr. Giampapa, assistant clinical professor of plastic and reconstructive surgery at the University of Medicine and Dentistry of New Jersey and author of five books, including the first medical textbook on antiaging medicine for aesthetic surgeons, joined Dr. Newman on the board.

William Amzallag, MD, became our director of product sciences and spokesman and adviser for Jeunesse in the European Union. He had the ideal background: decades of experience in the medical field and degrees in anesthesiology, intensive care, and Chinese medicine. Dr. Amzallag also became a member of the board, as did Donna Antarr, MD, whose expertise ranged from preventative and rejuvenation medicine and exercise physiology to the mind-body connection in wellness.

The expertise and brilliance of these four doctors, and others, would be essential for product development and training.

By the time we reached our fourth anniversary in 2013, we'd added another board member, Luis Martinez, MD, renowned for his expertise in regenerative, hormonal, and nutritional techniques that can repair and restore cellular functions as well as increase life expectancy. We'd opened twenty offices, employed two hundred people, and had two hundred thousand distributors in eighty-five countries. No wonder the Direct Selling Association gave us its ETHOS Rising Star Award in recognition of our growth, high standard of business excellence, and our spirit, dedication, and philanthropy.

At our September expo, the first international "We Are Generation Young" celebrations, some eight thousand distributors from thirty countries gathered in Thailand. In the Luminesce line, as part of what had evolved to become our Youth Enhancement System (YES), we added Luminesce Youth Restoring Cleanser, Luminesce Essential Body Renewal, and Luminesce Ultimate Lifting Masque.

Internationally, especially in the Far East, Jeunesse was unstoppable. But in 2014, it was the home market that enjoyed a phenomenal boost with Instantly Ageless™, a face cream whose benefits had to be seen to be believed. Unveiled at our Jeunesse University event in Orlando, Florida, a live on-stage demo wowed everyone.

The creator of the cream and a woman volunteer who had significant bags under her eyes took center stage. The audience eagerly watched as the cream was gently dabbed under one eye, while for comparison the other eye was left untouched. A transformation began within seconds. As the cream worked its magic and the under-eye bags visibly diminished until they almost completely disappeared, gasps of astonishment were followed by wild applause. In less than two minutes, a more toned, smoother looking complexion could be seen, a result that could last up to nine hours.

Distributors bought the cream like crazy, filmed their own before and after demos, and posted the demos online. Instantly Ageless instantly went viral. As word rapidly spread, the official company video on YouTube was viewed more than two million times, and distributor videos were watched millions more times. The viral videos created such a stir that national TV programs like *Inside Edition* and the *Rachel Ray Show* featured the product.

Instantly Ageless became a revenue generating powerhouse largely responsible for a boost in domestic sales within four months from $2.5 million a month to $15 million a month. More than fifty million applications of Instantly Ageless have since been sold, and numerous copycats jumped into the marketplace, which I guess is the sincerest form of flattery.

Our fifth anniversary event held in Macau in September 2014 was our largest ever. There was what we called a "ring of fire," a huge array of pulsating lights that formed the backdrop on the biggest stage we'd ever seen. Wendy and I walked out there, hand in hand, as nineteen giant screens projected our images and fourteen thousand distributors applauded, many excitedly waving their national flags. Temporarily blinded by the flashes of their phone cameras and deafened by blaring music, I realized what it must be like to be a rock star—well, an aging rock star maybe. It was an unforgettable moment that told us Jeunesse Global was on course for greater things.

At the same event, Cirque du Soleil acrobats performed a dazzling show high above the crowd, and we launched ZEN BODI™, a trio of weight management products designed to cut food cravings, burn fat, and build muscle, formulated and clinically tested by Dr. Antarr.

We thought it would be a great idea to send each distributor home with a bright red suitcase bearing the ZEN BODI logo and filled with samples of the products. It was quite a sight as thousands of identical suitcases were rolled through the airport. Maybe it was too striking a sight. The customs people couldn't miss it, and in some instances, they refused to let the products go through. Result: Thousands of suitcases were returned to us, covering the floor of a huge ballroom at the hotel. Products had to be repackaged so they could later be shipped to distributors.

By that point, we'd pulled in sales of about $350 million for the year, and Scott's on-stage proclamation that our vision was to achieve one billion dollars the next year may have seemed somewhat idealistic.

We closed out 2014 with global revenue of $419 million. Eighteen of our international markets recorded sales in excess of one million dollars a month, meeting the target we set when we opened our doors of having solid business in as many countries as possible to offset an economic downturn in any one country.

Our international expansion was carried out with us being acutely aware that US companies had a bad reputation for barnstorming into a foreign land and dictating they operate "the American way"—a big mistake guaranteed to offend citizens of those countries. We knew that the better approach was to adapt to local cultures and customs, recruit the best management team and distributors we could find in each country, and then listen to them. They would know their territory better than we did.

Paying attention to local input has been one of the main reasons for our global success, along with our prior experience with organizing logistics country by country for Fuel Freedom International. We knew what to do and what not to do, and we'd learned that if you don't do it right, you're unlikely to get a second chance.

We also learned that when working with diverse people and cultures, you have to develop a clear, cohesive strategy, efficiently execute it, and be flexible. In the interests of serving our distributors across all time zones we appointed five regional presidents (for Greater China, Europe and the Middle East, North America, Asia Pacific and Africa, and Japan) who not only look after their own regions but also routinely meet with us to discuss worldwide expansion.

When our sixth anniversary arrived in 2015, our independent sales force had grown to 550,000 in more than 120 countries, with thirty-two offices and forty distribution centers. And 2015 was the year in which our annual sales surpassed one billion dollars for the first time, achieving the goal Scott had announced in Macau the year before. What a monumental occasion that was—although with the target in sight, we'd worked so hard in the closing months of the year, we were too burned out to celebrate!

Acquiring other companies was not part of our business strategy until an opportunity came along to acquire the assets of MonaVie, another major player in the direct sales industry, a ten-year-old company based out of Salt Lake City that had a line of juice blends, energy drinks, and shake mixes. MonaVie had enjoyed phenomenal growth. Within four years of its start and after posting annual revenue of $855 million, it ranked eighteenth on the *Inc. 500* list of fastest-growing companies in the US. But its rapid ascent stalled and collapsed amid lawsuits and controversies. Distributors left and sales dramatically declined.

The acquisition made sense for us. The company's product line was complementary to ours, but its biggest asset was its distributor network, especially in Brazil, a country we eyed as part of our international expansion. Top leadership had remained loyal, even though the company was on the verge of collapse. The key product, MonaVie Active™, was a drink designed to help support joint mobility and flexibility in a blend of vitamins A, C, and E, plant-based glucosamine, and nineteen fruits, including the Brazilian acai berry. It had a huge following of consumers on a monthly auto-ship program, which was an attractive proposition, and to this day it continues to sell very well. So we stepped in to merge the business with Jeunesse and expand the opportunity for its distributors.

We ran Jeunesse out of a large warehouse we'd previously renovated and turned into office space for Fuel Freedom International. It was functional but not the most comfortable or prestigious building. So in 2016 we moved into a new 130,000-square-foot facility in Lake Mary, Florida, that was more in keeping with the needs and image of a billion-dollar operation. We kept the original building for shipping and receiving. We also opened a 30,000-plus square-foot "Jeunesse West" facility near Salt Lake City.

The plan was to have a gala ribbon cutting event for the new headquarters attended by Diamond Directors from around the world to coincide with our annual expo early October. We went all out to make it an event to be remembered. We partially drained the lake next to the building to use it for staging, and we set up food tents for an evening of dining and entertainment. Our creative team put together a superb laser show to be projected on the building.

It was to be a million-dollar extravaganza—until Hurricane Matthew had a different idea. Matthew, a Category 5 hurricane, skirted the Florida coastline bringing the very real danger that it could swing inland at any time. The state of Florida declared a state of emergency on October 3 and urged a million and a half residents to evacuate as winds of up to 80 mph brought down trees and power lines. A federal declaration followed on Thursday, October 6, the day of the scheduled ribbon cutting. It was obvious that the show could not go on. We weren't the only company to be affected. Walt Disney World Resort closed its doors for only the fourth time in its forty-five-year history.

The Jeunesse event organizers were concerned that the hurricane would devastate their entire setup and quickly moved into action to tear it down before the fury of Matthew tore it down. Our team went to extraordinary lengths to make sure distributors had flashlights and food in their hotel rooms. Although we were forced to cancel some of the expo events, we were able to hold general sessions at the Orlando Convention Center on Saturday and Sunday. The creative team showed a sense of humor by designing a giant umbrella graphic that was projected onto the new corporate headquarters.

That was one way to blow one million dollars! Not that we got the worst of it. The hurricane caused twelve deaths in Florida and $2.77 billion of damage.

That year we were the only company in the direct selling industry to be listed on the *Inc. 500* list, and we picked up thirteen Stevie Awards from the American Business Awards organization. We also launched Nevo™, a refreshing energy drink, in lemon ginger, mixed berry, peach mango, and acai grape flavors.

At our annual Emerald Experience incentive trip in Maui, we kicked off 2017 with the announcement that an Olympics venue in Brazil had been renamed Jeunesse Arena. This major promotional endeavor was recognition of Brazil as a fast-growing and extremely important market for us. The nineteen thousand-seat arena in Rio de Janeiro had hosted marquee events, including the 2016 Olympics gymnastics competition, the NBA Global Games, and Disney on Ice, as well as major performers like Beyoncé and Paul McCartney and would continue to be a major venue in Rio de Janeiro.

To celebrate our first anniversary in Brazil, we held an event of our own at the arena featuring a performance by musical artist Anitta, three-time winner of Best Brazilian Act at the MTV Europe Music Awards. Driving up to the arena and seeing the Jeunesse name above the entrance for the first time was quite a spine-tingling experience.

Not long afterward, we supported our distributors in South Korea, the world's third largest direct-selling market, by negotiating a sponsorship deal with FC Seoul, the country's most popular soccer team. Jeunesse signage at their home field, Seoul World Cup Stadium, was highly visible to the 66,000 fans at the games and the large audience of fans watching on TV.

We stepped into the world of cosmetics with a brand cocreated by a celebrity makeup artist. Called NV, this brand was designed to create a professional airbrushed look for its users while being formulated without oil, parabens, sulfates, or phthalates. The line launched with NV Primer, nine shades of NV BB Perfecting Mist Foundation, and NV Bronzer.

Our substantial growth was recognized the same year when we were presented with the *Direct Selling News* Bravo Growth Award, and Scott was named one of the industry's "Forces Under 40."

Because of our growth, we needed to expand our annual expo convention into five regions, and fifty thousand distributors showed up for events in Macau, Bangkok, Milan, Sao Paulo, and Orlando. They all got to experience firsthand the addition of Luminesce HydraShield Mask to our bestselling skin care line. This coconut bio cellulose sheet mask includes our patented APT-200 ingredient and is infused with antioxidant-rich shea butter and ultra-hydrating Asian grass root extract.

In the supplements category, we came out with MIND™, a product featuring silk protein hydrolysate, which supports memory, and L-Theanine, which helps reduce mental distraction.

The year 2018 was a banner year for us in many ways. Most significantly, we achieved global annual sales of $1.46 billion—a $164 million, 12.3 percent increase over the previous year, and September was our best-ever month with sales surging past the two hundred-million-dollar mark.

We rose to the position of number thirteen on the DSN Global 100 list, and the Jeunesse EXPO World Tour attracted more than sixty-two thousand distributors in five regions of the world, 24 percent higher attendance than 2017.

Among a total of 141 corporate awards, for the fifth consecutive year, we made the *Inc. 5000* list of fastest-growing private companies in America. We were also named an Inc. Private Titan, a designation given to large privately owned companies that continue to perform year after year. Campden Research, a division of Campden Wealth Research, a global research and networking organization for high net worth families, announced we were the #1 Fastest Growing Mid-Size Family Business. And we picked up the gold for Company Growth of the Year in the SVUS business awards.

We extended membership of the scientific advisory board to include Yan Bin Ma, MD, who, during her thirty-five-year career, has specialized in integrating Chinese and Western medicine, alternative medicine, and natural therapy. Dr. Ma has extensive experience in teaching and research at the Chinese Academy of Medical Sciences in Beijing, and since becoming a Canadian citizen, has founded an alternative medicine clinic, focusing on autoimmune disorders.

To keep up with the needs of a growing international sales force, we broadened our range of products and also supported distributors with special promotions in their home markets.

On the product front, we entered the haircare market with the RVL™ Advanced Hair Care System, a shampoo, conditioner, and scalp treatment that became a Pure Beauty Global Beauty Awards Winner the following year. RVL Scalp Infusion Treatment and RVL Multi-Perfecting Leave-In Conditioner are infused with HPT-6™, a revolutionary polypeptide technology created by Dr. Newman.

We launched RevitaBlū™. Developed by neurophysiologist Christian Drapeau, MSc., RevitaBlū is a blend of sea buckthorn fruit harvested from high on the Tibetan plateau, blue-green algae, aloe vera, and beta glucan with coconut water powder, ingredients that help nourish and support your body. Drapeau, who has achieved global recognition for his pioneering work in plant-based stem cell research and regenerative medicine, also joined the scientific advisory board.

We also came out with Naära, a drink that uses patented and clinically studied hydrolyzed collagen that supports the skin from the inside out, helping battle the natural decrease of collagen in the body.

On the promotional front, we sponsored major soccer teams in Ukraine (FC Dynamo Kiev), and in Turkey (Galatasaray SK). In Argentina we sponsored Superliga Argentina, the premier soccer league in the country.

Our Nevo™ Energy Drink became the Official Energy Drink of Carnival in Brazil, and the brand was also attached to the SESC volleyball clubs. In South Korea, we sponsored Olympic speed skater Kim Min Seok, winner of silver and bronze medals at the 2018 Winter Games.

In 2019, we broke into the increasingly popular functional water market with the release of MX_2O™, a dietary supplement with more than seventy trace minerals and black organic fulvic and humic acids, formulated to help users, as our tagline says, "live life to the max."

During the Jeunesse EXPO World Tour, we rolled out E•VŌK™, five proprietary essential oil blends selected from five continents and crafted by Dr. Amzallag in conjunction with a renowned botanical master perfumer. Our first durable goods product, the E•VŌK Nebulizing Diffuser, can be used to disperse the oils to maximize their benefits.

But beyond these major expo events, we stage more than three hundred shows a year across the globe. Many network marketing companies have their distributors travel to the corporate home office, but we make a big investment in time and money going to the people. At some events, we have a special themed dinner for top leaders. One year we all got dressed up in Roaring Twenties clothes. Another year, it was snow wear. Another time, Romany gypsies. We know how to have fun, but more often than not, the highlight for us is when person after person gets up on stage and sometimes tearfully, sometimes joyfully, talks about how Jeunesse has transformed their lives.

Cliff Walker from the UK, who's a Diamond Director, loves to tell the story about the day someone told him about the Jeunesse opportunity. "We'd just had a traditional business go belly-up, and we had lost almost everything. Then I was contacted about a new business someone named Randy Ray was launching."

Amazingly, Cliff was looking at my business card sitting on his desk. He'd met us some time before when he was marketing an online video program. What a coincidence. It was meant to be. I got a phone call and heard an unmistakable British accent.

"Randy, it's Cliff Walker from the UK."

After I explained to Cliff what we were doing, he didn't hesitate. He and wife Bev packed their bags, and along with their dog Bella, they jumped on a plane to the States, leaving everything else behind.

Cliff recalls that we invited them to share Thanksgiving with us— even though they're British. He likes the fact that I call a spade a spade, and he claims that everyone loves me and my jokes, which is something I find very hard to believe.

When Lyndon Biernoff decided to come out of retirement, he spent a frustrating two years seeking the right network marketing company. After hearing about Jeunesse, he flew to Orlando from his home in Australia to check us out. "I walked into a boardroom and there were two people I mistook for the office cleaners, but they were actually the owners, Wendy and Randy."

Once he realized his error, we proceeded to have what he describes as a "strange but refreshing" meeting. Lyndon is someone else who seems to have been charmed by what he describes as my "constant stream of jokes and political incorrectness" and my transparency. We obviously had shared values, and we connected. Luckily,

Lyndon decided to join the office cleaners and has become extremely successful, reaching the position of Double Diamond Director.

Time and again we hear distributors enthuse about their life transformations. Australian Emerald Director Angela Lucente says Jeunesse "has helped me regain my purpose in life and dream big again."

Diamond Directors Paula Pritchard and Kathy Robbins say, "At the end of our lives, we will be able to look back and see the impact of lives well-lived and the lives we have changed."

Distributors agree that our products, first and foremost, are what drive the Jeunesse business. We've always believed that unique products that deliver what they promise inspire distributor and customer loyalty. The products make those who use them look younger and feel younger, and people keep using them because they work. One woman even told me that Luminesce helped her skin so much she wished she could take a bath in it!

Love of products that help people live more youthful and fuller lives makes it easy for distributors to recommend them to others. We make it even easier by embracing cutting-edge high-tech marketing tools. For us, it was the natural thing to do. We've been at the forefront of technological innovation since my days developing a program for the Space Shuttle launch system and, with Wendy, creating and marketing medical software and hardware.

In an ever-growing social media world, we've made it simple for our distributors to communicate with leads across the globe. Through J-Social, part of our J-Marketing platform, a distributor can interact with and connect people to their own personalized website via their smartphone, Facebook, or any social media environment. We create the highest quality tools so they don't have to.

We don't outsource very much. We prefer to handle internally everything from full-scale IT and logistics, customer service, and shipping, to event planning, creative marketing, and communications. We have gone out of our way to avoid an ivory tower mentality and have an open-door environment where employees at every level can feel free to share their thoughts. We appreciate individual contributions and love to promote from within. Employees stay with us: 135 people have been with Jeunesse for longer than five years because they feel they belong to a community where they make a difference.

We've always taken pride in very simple, clear messaging and a culture based on our core values and mission statement: The Jeunesse Family creates positive impact in the world by helping people look and feel young while empowering each other to unleash our potential.

Our employees know that and our distributors know that. Our personal and corporate integrity form our greatest considerations. A major objective is to create an opportunity that is sustainable and compliant with the ever-changing regulatory climate. We believe in doing things the right way, and we place a large value on education and the prevention of policy violations.

In 2015, our compliance department was one of the first in the industry to launch a virtual training system, and it continues to create resources that take the guesswork out of what to say and what to do when marketing Jeunesse. With a network of 675,000 independent distributors and growing, we can't prevent all violations, but we strive to focus on retention of distributors rather than on termination, depending on the nature of the violation. Because we recognize the value in leading with integrity and embracing compliance, we have broken the norms. For five consecutive years, the Direct Selling Association has recognized Jeunesse as one of only a handful of member companies in their annual Code Communications Initiative, which encourages and promotes education on the Code of Ethics.

Our growth has certainly raised our visibility, and fortunately, it has brought a lot of favorable attention with a slew of awards from business organizations and the media.

The Stevie Awards presented annually by the American Business Awards organization is widely considered the Oscars of the business world. Jeunesse has been honored five times with The Grand Stevie, the most prestigious title of all, for winning the most awards in a year. We've won Management Team of the Year awards in US and International categories eight times and Founding Team of the Year four times. Wendy has collected a dozen awards in various Woman of the Year categories. She's been named five times in each of the Female Executive of the Year, Female Entrepreneur of the Year, and Lifetime Achievement categories and twice as Maverick of the Year. I've been honored six times in the Executive of the Year category in America and internationally. And I have twice been given the Lifetime Achievement Award. Scott is a seven-time recipient of the Maverick of the Year Award.

On the product side, we have been presented with Stevies for Best New Product of the Year for Instantly Ageless, Nevo, NV, Luminesce HydraShield Mask, RVL Scalp Infusion Treatment, and the suite of business management software: Jworld, Jdrive and Jcloud.

Wendy is a true force in the industry. On top of all of the Stevie awards, she has been honored three times by *Direct Selling News* as One of the Most Influential Women in Direct Selling. In Women World Awards, she has earned thirteen titles including Champion of the Year, Woman of the Year, Female Entrepreneur of the Year, and Female Executive of the Year.

In 2017, we were finalists in the EY Entrepreneur of the Year competition and NETCOO *Next Economy Magazine* presented the company with its International Company of the Year 2018–2019 award.

Our in-house marketing team has garnered hundreds of awards for the top-class brochures, videos, mailers, mobile apps, and websites they have created, honored in programs such as the Telly Awards, MarCom Awards, Communicator Awards, and AVA Digital Awards. Our chief marketing officer Mark Patterson has won the Stevies Marketing Executive of the Year award eight times.

We like to receive awards and we love to give awards.

If there's one thing that Jeunesse does better than just about any other company, it's organize incentive trips. In 2019, a total of 19,795 distributors traveled with us to celebrate their achievements. For many of them they're trips they would never get to do on their own, and we pride ourselves on doing more than the average company would do.

We once took twelve thousand people from Greater China to Switzerland. The tour company had to stretch to handle so many people. Another time we had four cruise ships set sail from Barcelona— all full of Jeunesse distributors. Two years in a row we filled the Four Seasons Hotel in Bora Bora in French Polynesia.

There was an unforgettable Arabian Nights experience out in the desert of Dubai during which our people rode camels and fell into the sand dunes. You name it, we've probably done it!

Not every trip goes as smoothly as we'd like. We had a few thousand people fly to California, mostly from the Far East, to embark on an Alaskan cruise. Unfortunately, a couple hundred distributors weren't allowed on board because they hadn't gotten the visa they needed for a port of call in Canada. We could have just said sorry, that's too bad. But they'd earned a travel reward, and a travel reward they were going to get. Our team scrambled to get them all on flights to Cabo San Lucas in Mexico. They ended up having a warm weather vacation instead of a cold weather vacation. Of course, all their clothes were suitable for Alaska, not Mexico!

Over the years we've been to places that are on bucket lists for many people. We've gone from the beaches of Hawaii to the mountains of Switzerland, from the Serengeti Plains in Africa to the Taj Mahal in India. We've taken people to European capitals as varied as Athens, Rome, Madrid, Dublin, Prague, and Budapest. We've voyaged to the Greek Isles, Tahiti, Dubai, Bali, Indonesia, and Australia. We've cruised the Mediterranean and the coast of Brazil. In the Caribbean, we've visited Jamaica, the Bahamas, and the Dominican Republic.

Often, Wendy and I have traveled with our distributors so we can share the experience and get to know them better. They're such a passionate, high-energy group of people who come to our events from all around the world. They like the feeling of being together, and they keep each other motivated. From day one, we were determined to have a close relationship with them because we knew what it was like to be in their shoes.

I once arrived in Taiwan on what turned out to be a national holiday, so no work could be done. It also happened to be the first day of bullet train service between Taichung and Taipei. "Let's go for lunch," I said to Double Diamond Director Samson Li and a group in a spur-of-the-minute decision.

"You're so spontaneous, always ready to try something new," Samson told me. He also said, "Sometimes it takes the heart and compassion of a little kid to empower others."

Really? A little kid? Me?

We've celebrated all manner of events, even being witnesses in Taiwan at the wedding of Double Diamond Director Jason Chiang and his bride Carin in a ceremony in front of eight hundred guests at the Grand Hotel Taipei. We were particularly honored that they named their daughter Jeunesse, and Jason says that becoming a distributor changed his life, saving him from debt.

There are people we can count on to be near the front of almost every event, even those attended by thousands of distributors. I make a point of looking out into the crowd to see if I can spot Emerald Directors John Payne and his wife Ahleyce Tan from Malaysia no matter where we are in the world. If I don't see this beautiful couple right away, I have to confess, I'm a little sad until I locate their big smiles and displays of infectious enthusiasm. They are such a welcome sight in the sea of faces.

The international aspect of the Jeunesse business, as well as our spirit, is what appeals to many of our leaders. Says Craig Schulze, a Diamond Director in Melbourne, Australia, "The Jeunesse platform has allowed me to travel the world and build a business in a hundred countries. It has been the most rewarding business adventure of my life and connects deeply with my values and heart."

Double Diamond Director Helen Zhang agrees. "Jeunesse brings together likeminded people from all over the world. Health is our common language and happiness is our common goal."

We've never calculated how many miles we've personally flown, but Wendy and I each have more than four million miles with both Delta and United and more than a million each with American. We also fly Emirates a lot. I like to say my current home is seat 6A. The fourteen-year-old Randy dreamed of traveling and meeting people from other cultures, but it has gone beyond my wildest dreams.

We've learned a lot about different cultures around the world. We're like the mom and dad of a huge multicultural, multigenerational global family of distributors.

And their success is our success.

Chapter 8

Secrets of Success

It's a business for people who want to break loose from a humdrum nine-to-five routine and aren't afraid to go for it.

How did you do it? That's the question Wendy and I are asked more than anything else. How did we build a billion-dollar company so quickly from scratch? We like to say, "We did the same thing we've always done. We put our heads down and went to work."

That's a big part of it. There's no such thing as overnight success. You have to pay your dues. You acquire knowledge from your experience. You learn from the things that you did right and even more from the things you did wrong. No one is perfect. Hopefully, you become smart enough to avoid making the same mistake twice.

Let me talk specifically about the network marketing industry, which boasts worldwide sales of close to two hundred billion dollars. It's an industry that attracts a lot of women, generally because it has been seen as a way of generating part-time income, but also because of female-focused products like skincare and cosmetics that are demonstrable and consumable. Of the 118 million independent representatives across the globe, 75 percent are women.

Network marketing is a highly effective person-to-person method of moving products from the manufacturer direct to the consumer, in effect cutting out the middleman. Instead of paying the middleman, independent distributors, who mostly operate out of their homes, participate in a generous commission-earning structure based on product sales by others they sponsor in their network, the people those people sponsor, and so on, multiple levels deep.

With reputable companies like Jeunesse, you can start a business with little or no money, sell products, and recruit distributors in most countries of the world—all from your own home. What other industry offers opportunities like that?

To find a network marketing company that's right for you, there are some basic questions I suggest you ask. First, it makes sense to have a passionate connection to the company's products. Ask yourself these questions about the products: Are they life-changing? Are they innovative? Are they unique? Are they demonstrable? That is, do you see or feel a benefit? Are they consumable, so customers keep coming back for more? Are they based on sound scientific research or endorsed by reputable scientists, doctors, or nutritionists? Does the company have a wide range of products?

What about the company itself? How long has it been in existence? Is it well-funded? Is there a qualified, experienced management team? What level of support do they provide to distributors in the field? Has the company or its leadership been honored by industry organizations and the media? Does the company enforce its policies and procedures to make sure distributors conduct themselves ethically?

What about the owners? What kind of track record of success do they have? Are they accessible? Do they take the time to meet distributors and show them hope, possibility, respect, humility, and love? Do they have heart and compassion?

Once you've found a company that has the right criteria, it's up to you. In many ways, you run your own business. Remember, you're in business for yourself but not by yourself because you have the support of the company you chose, the person who sponsored you, and the network of distributors above you, in your upline.

Network marketing is a business in which independent distributors can achieve whatever goals they set for themselves. They're not hired by the company. On the contrary, they choose the company they want to work with. They choose how many hours they want to work and where they want to work. They can work after they've put the kids to bed or when they return home from their ordinary day job. Or on the weekends. Distributors pick which products they want to promote and who they're going to approach.

It's a business for people who want to break loose from a humdrum nine-to-five routine and aren't afraid to go for it. You don't need to make a big investment buying a ton of inventory or renting office space and equipment. You don't need a PhD. You don't need any experience because you can learn as you earn and generate more income than a PhD, if that's what you want.

You also don't need to put together a sophisticated five-year business plan or create beautifully designed marketing materials. That's what the company does. What you do need is a willingness to learn and work hard. You need the drive and determination to succeed, and you need to make good use of all of the materials and guidance provided by the company. Why reinvent the wheel when the company has put together a formula for success?

People are individual with individual goals and dreams. Some want to achieve something specific, maybe make enough money to buy a car or put their kids through private school. Others set their sights high and are willing to expend extraordinary effort to make it to the top. We have distributors who are happy to make pocket money, those who make a good full-time income, and those who make even more than a good full-time income. It's their choice.

While anybody can succeed, I recognize that it's not a business for everybody. From my years of experience, I've identified three kinds of people who join a network marketing company: the climbers, the campers, and the quitters.

The climbers are the people who won't let anything get in their way. Nothing stops them. No matter what obstacles are thrown in front of them, they knock them down and keep on climbing. They've seen what others have accomplished, and they have their eyes firmly set on reaching the pinnacle.

The campers are people who start the business and who take a break after doing a certain amount and getting just so far. They're happy where they are, comfortable working a few hours a week to collect a commission check that supplements the lifestyle they want or enables them to pay for certain short-term goals.

The quitters are those who sign up as distributors and give it a go but aren't totally committed. Then they quit. Afterward they say, "I tried it, and it didn't work." The reality is that *they* didn't work. Perhaps they thought it would be easy and didn't appreciate how much work is necessary to really make a go of it. But again, it's their choice.

Some people feel that you have to be a gregarious, outgoing salesperson to be successful. Nothing could be further from reality. I have that kind of personality, but Wendy doesn't. She will be the first to tell you that her biggest challenge was her shyness. She's always been shy, and in some ways, she still is, even though she's the cofounder of and a major driving force behind Jeunesse. Years ago, when she was a teacher, Wendy's shyness was so extreme that she'd break out in hives if the school superintendent or school principal came into the classroom to observe her teach. In their presence, she found it difficult to talk to her students.

When we first became involved in network marketing and got up on stage, Wendy couldn't speak. She held my hand tight and let me do all the talking. Now she stands up and confidently addresses audiences of any size, even tens of thousands of people in auditoriums and stadiums. She persevered and learned how to overcome her shyness and her fear of public speaking.

It's a great example, especially since communicating with others—making individual sales calls, never mind public speaking—is a big issue in this industry. Many people think they can't do it because they're afraid to call someone to have a sales conversation. And that's all it is really, a conversation. But they're hesitant to tell someone about a product they love, even though doing so is no different than recommending a great book, a movie, or a new restaurant. They get tongue-tied and fumble their words, terrified of being rejected.

What I always say is, embrace rejection. It's fine if people say no today. They might say yes tomorrow. Maybe you just approached them at the wrong time. And each time someone says no, it just brings you closer to someone who will say yes. Move on. There are plenty of people who need our products and will want to try the products. For the congenitally shy who feel that they can't make personal contact, we have dynamite social media tools that empower distributors to communicate very effectively and break down the barriers.

Our greatest pleasure is helping the most unlikely of people rise from nothing to become shining examples of entrepreneurship at its very best.

Let me give you some examples.

Tina Hu moved from China to the US in search of the American dream. Without a strong educational background, she worked as a waitress and a maid. She was barely making it, but she aspired to do more in life. She came up to me at an event in California and in halting English made it clear she was done with the dead-end jobs she'd held for ten years.

"Can I really do this?" she asked.

"Absolutely," I said.

"But I don't know what to say to people."

"All you have to do is walk up to someone and ask if they would like to feel younger. Who doesn't want to look younger? When they say yes, you tell them that we have products for that."

She said she could do that. And she did, ignoring people who discouraged her. She has done so well, she achieved the position of Triple Diamond Director. "I turned from a woman who had nothing into someone who has wealth and free time."

Lisa Griggs-Riordan was a single mom on welfare living in her car with three children. When the car was repossessed, they slept on the floor of an empty room in a friend's house. Lisa wanted to earn an extra five hundred dollars, an amount she felt would give her a measure of freedom and at the very least allow her to buy Tickle Me Elmos for her kids.

She told me it was the darkest and most disappointing time in her life.

She found my life story inspiring and went to work.

"I've been able to regain my dignity as a woman and a mother and escape poverty. My children and I are first-time homeowners and have traveled the world as a family. And I have been able to give back."

When we were on a visit to Malaysia, one of our distributors told us about a home for battered women and their children. There is not a single reason on God's Earth for a man to physically and mentally abuse a woman or a child. It's just incomprehensible to me that a man could do that. We visited the home in Kuala Lumpur, the country's capital, and heard about some bad situations. We saw women with broken arms and bruised, swollen faces, and we saw the despair in their eyes as they hugged their children close to them. We were moved to make a donation of one hundred thousand Malaysian Ringgit.

But our visit had an even more meaningful outcome. Two of the women who were sheltered there were curious about our business. Like Tina Hu, they wondered if it was something they could do to improve their lives and the lives of their children. We encouraged them, telling them it was a way to start a new, independent life and make good money to support themselves and their kids. They did better than that, way better. Fast forward a few years. Both of them became top leaders and were easily able to pay their daughters' way through college in the US.

There are many who come from similar desperate backgrounds who are now doing extremely well financially. What they also have in common is a willingness to listen and learn. They don't think they know it all and they don't bring preconceived notions from other business experiences. We tell them to listen to the people in their upline who have been successful and follow their example.

I've founded three companies that have appeared on the *Inc. 500* list of Fastest Growing Private Companies in America. Jeunesse has made that list five times, so I do know a few things about building a successful business.

When people ask me why Jeunesse has done so well, I tell them that we have outstanding products and a superb compensation plan, and we ship to more than 145 countries. It's true that a lot of companies can make similar statements. What makes us different is the heartfelt relationship we have with our distributors. We really care about them and want them to do well. They're like family to us—one very big family. Wendy and I strongly feel that to be truly successful, you have to have a servant's heart. It's not all about you, it's about others.

If you can help other people achieve what they want in life, you will automatically achieve what you want. Adopt that mindset and you will succeed. It's all about how many people you can help.

What else can you do to build a network of your own? Here are some tips.

Work at your own pace. Some people get off to a fast start. They operate at a frenetic tempo and don't stop. And that's great. But sometimes slow and steady gets you there. You just have to be willing to learn and focus, know what your goals are, and keep going. Don't give up. We have people who have been in Jeunesse nine years before making it as a Diamond, and the rewards are well worth the time it took. This is the kind of business anyone can do at their own pace, so don't let other people distract you.

Keep the faith. Ignore the naysayers. It's a sad fact of life that there will be people who always try to undermine you. They'll come to you all the time and question why you are doing this or that. You need to decide what your goals are, what you want to achieve. The only people who lose are the ones who give up. If you believe it will happen, it will happen. Ming Lee is a fine example. "Every time someone tore me down, I gritted my teeth and kept going, even through all the pain they caused me. I never lashed back. With no family to support me in America, those times were especially difficult." Ming, who hails from China, rose to the position of Double Diamond Director. "The life I lead today is so meaningful. I'm able to use the blessings that God bestowed upon me to help others."

Spend your time wisely. There is at least one of life's riches that we all share, and that's having twenty-four hours a day. It's what you do with those 1,440 minutes that makes the difference. You have direct control over how you invest your time, so invest it wisely. Plan and manage your time.

Don't get too smart for your own good. It's easy to learn all the fine points of a particular product and seek to impress prospects with your wealth of knowledge. My advice is to avoid turning the firehose on them. Tell them as much as they need to know and no more. If they have specific questions, answer them. And remember that quite often, less is more. If you swamp potential distributors with too much information, you might scare them off. They might think there's no way they could emulate you. Keep it simple and duplicable.

Get your priorities right. How important to you is your network marketing business? Can you sacrifice five or ten hours of watching TV a week? Can you go to bed one hour later or get up one hour earlier and spend that time on your own business? What about working on the weekend? It's up to you. The decision is yours and yours alone. But generally, those people who put in the extra effort are those who earn the extra income.

Be professional. While you might be working from home and on a part-time basis, that's no reason to conduct yourself in a slapdash "anything goes" manner. Jeunesse provides first-class products, materials, and support, so why not represent the company in a classy, ethical, responsible manner.

Be persistent and patient. Everything isn't always going to go your way. There will be people who reject your approaches or ridicule your business opportunity. Sometimes, those closest to you—family, relatives, and friends—can be the most skeptical. Don't let their negativity rub off on you. They may feel threatened by the person you are about to become. And don't give up if you're not an overnight success. Do you really think anyone is an overnight success? The poet Henry Wadsworth Longfellow said, "Perseverance is a great element of success. If you only knock long enough and loud enough at the gate, you are sure to wake up somebody."

Give praise where it's due. As you grow your network and rise to higher leadership positions, celebrate everyone for achieving what they want to achieve. Don't turn off a solid performer and make her feel like a failure because she's not doing as well as you. If someone sets a lesser goal and achieves it, it's reason for celebration.

On a personal level, Wendy says that one thing she's learned is that if you can't change something, don't stew over it. Don't get upset. Let it go. But there again, she's a lot smarter than me. She also says you need to learn to schedule time for yourself because it's all too easy to be consumed by the business and work nonstop. Of course, this is from the woman I catch sending texts and emails in the middle of the night!

We've both worked all our lives, and it's hard for us to stop. We've tried to retire three times but never quite figured out how to do it. In our "retirement," we once built a house and took several dream vacations overseas, but when the biggest decision was what to have for breakfast, we knew we were in trouble. That wasn't us. We had to get back to work.

In running the business, we tend to trust our own instincts. It's served us well over the years. Although we firmly believe in getting input and weighing the viewpoints of others, we've found that if our gut tells us something is right or wrong, we're usually right. We've learned that it doesn't pay to be wishy-washy and waver with the wind.

Another reason for my personal success is my determination and strength of conviction. In the scriptures, it says, "I will fear no evil: for you are with me." (NRSV, Psalms, 23:4) I haven't feared anything. In the darkest moments, in the bleakest times in my life, I have fallen back on those words. I have always said, no matter how bad a situation becomes, it is no big deal. I will get through it. In my mind, nothing was going to stop me. If God didn't want me to do something, then it wasn't going to happen. My faith has kept me strong.

We have been truly blessed, and that's why we decided to share those blessings with the less fortunate.

Chapter 9

Giving Back

One heart. One hope. One mission.

My dad always said, if you've been blessed, you need to bless others. Otherwise your blessing can go away. I've been blessed. And I want to bless others. Considering where I came from and all the strikes against me early in life, I'm one of the luckiest people on the planet.

Because I know what it's like to grow up poor without halfway decent clothes, a nice bed to sleep in, or food to eat, I have a special place in my heart for kids born into dire circumstances. They didn't ask to be here; they can't help themselves. But we can help them. We can give back.

That's why in 2012, Wendy and I created Jeunesse Kids™, a 501(c)(3) nonprofit charitable foundation. Our mission is "Empowering communities to give children a brighter future." We work with that mission on each of the five continents where we operate. Our motto: "One heart. One hope. One mission." Jeunesse underwrites all the costs associated with running the foundation, so every penny that's donated goes directly to help good causes. Donations don't get swallowed up by administrative costs.

At first, we partnered with a company to provide millions of meals to children in countries as far apart as the Philippines and Uganda where there were 1.7 million orphans under the age of fifteen whose parents had either been wiped out by AIDS or by the brutal regime of the crazy Ugandan dictator Idi Amin.

But it became obvious to us that feeding kids was not enough. It's all very well to give them food today, but what about tomorrow? It's more important to show them and their families how to fend for themselves so they can feed themselves in the future. We wanted to build something sustainable for the long haul. So we searched for a reputable organization that shared our values and with which we could partner.

That led us to Craig Kielburger, a remarkable man who launched the charity Free the Children in 1995 when he was just twelve years old. Craig was struck by the tragic story of a boy his age who lived half a world away in Pakistan. Iqbal Masih's desperate parents had used him as collateral for a loan when he was four years old. They needed the money to pay for surgery for his mother, but they failed to repay the loan, and the little boy was sold into slavery, forced to work more than twelve hours a day weaving carpets. He was beaten, abused, and chained to his loom. At the age of ten, Iqbal escaped and became an advocate for children's rights, giving many carpet worker children the courage to leave their owners. In retaliation, he was shot dead at the age of twelve.

Inspired to take action, Craig rallied ten schoolfriends and his older brother Marc. From his parents' living room, they launched Free the Children with the ambitious goal of freeing children from slavery. Adult activists and government officials were spurred into action, with the result that sweatshops and brothels that exploited youngsters were shut down. Later, Craig discovered that their success was short-lived. Rescued kids were pulled back into servitude. Changing a culture of slavery was not so easy. To end child labor, they would need to break the cycle of extreme poverty.

Free the Children has evolved to become WE Charity, an organization highly rated by independent organizations that evaluate charities. In 2017, it was the first recipient of *Good Housekeeping* magazine's Humanitarian Seal. WE Charity's development model delivered exactly what we were looking for: a way to empower impoverished families to learn ways to sustain themselves.

When Scott talked with Marc and Craig, there was an instant meeting of minds. Our values were aligned. Their hearts were in the right place, and they wanted to operate their charity with minimal administrative fees, putting the money to best use.

Together we came up with a plan to adopt one village a year in various countries. The strategy was to establish a covenant with a village. We'd provide vital funding, leadership, and support; the villagers would pledge to work hard to capitalize on everything we provided. The goal was to establish a totally self-reliant community within five to eight years. It was not a handout; it was a hand-up.

Unveiled in September 2014 at EXPO 5, our major convention in Macau, the collaboration was kickstarted by a $350,000 fundraising drive.

When we adopt a village, WE Charity implements its proven WE Villages development model that focuses on five pillars of impact: education, clean water, health, food, and opportunity. The idea is to supply the tools and resources along with providing skills and capacity building to empower these folks to lift their families and their communities out of poverty.

First, the WE team, partnering with local doctors and medical professionals, completes a community health scan and evaluates what targeted health interventions may be needed. Second, they check the water supply. Where does it come from? Is it clean or contaminated? Do they get enough water?

Next, what's their food supply? Is it agriculture or aquaculture—farming off the land or fishing in a river? Is that sustainable? How long does their food supply last?

So far, we've adopted seven villages in four countries on three continents: two in China, two in Kenya, two in India, and one in Ecuador. Wendy and I, along with members of the Jeunesse family, have visited villages on what we call "Bringing Hope" trips.

We've built classrooms and hired teachers to teach in them. We've delivered hygiene and health education and mobile health clinics that visit villages. We've drilled wells and installed hand-washing stations and latrines. We've shown local people how to farm and fish more efficiently to boost the nutritional status of their communities. And we've initiated programs to teach them how to generate and manage an income stream.

China

Our first partnership in 2014 was the nine hundred-year-old community of Dao Lazui in northeastern China where 90 percent of 3,300 villagers survived on less than two dollars a day. The school was crumbling. Clean water was hard to find. Health was negatively impacted by lack of knowledge. Farming was unproductive.

The involvement of Jeunesse Kids has transformed their lives.

The village school now boasts a modern classroom for each grade, one through five. In addition, we built a library and accommodations and offices for two teachers. We also installed a kitchen so the children can be fed as soon as they arrive at school in the morning and before they leave in the afternoon because there may not be food at home.

We've completed a borehole that delivers water to a significant portion of the wider community, and by doing so, we have been able to stave off waterborne illnesses and disease. Dao Lazui no longer depends on the uncertainty of rainfall to harvest its crops. A reliable irrigation system has enabled them to grow a variety of vegetables of higher quality and in higher quantity than they were capable of before, doubling the income of local farmers. Younger family members who fled to the big cities are returning to invest in the land that has been handed down for generations.

As part of a Bringing Hope trip, Wendy and I visited Dao Lazui in December 2015 to see the transformation with our own eyes. It was a trip that almost didn't happen. First, it took almost a full day to travel from Orlando to Beijing, and that was the easy part. When we got there, our WE Charity partners seriously considered cancelling the journey to the village because the weather had turned so foul. It was windy and freezing cold. The roads were icy and treacherous. The four-and-a-half-hour drive got tougher the closer we got to the village, and we almost skidded off the road several times. But we made it.

We knew it would be cold and had provided comfortable Jeunesse-branded jackets for everyone in our group. But we'd never experienced anything like this weather. It was far worse than the harsh winters of my childhood in Tennessee. It was so cold it was difficult to speak. It was as if your lungs were frozen. This was contrasted sharply by the warmth of our welcome. Little kids lined up to greet us holding signs, waving, cheering, and singing. I couldn't believe the lightweight clothes and the rubber shoes they wore in the snow and biting cold.

Something else struck me right away: There were a lot of young kids, but with them were a lot of elderly people who looked far too old to be their parents. We learned that the parents had been sent to work in factories the other side of the country, leaving the grandparents to handle parenting duties. The kids might get to see their parents once a year.

We had brought backpacks for the kids that were loaded with pencils, paper, and other basic school supplies. But when we tried to hand them out, the kids didn't want to touch them. They looked and backed off. We asked one of the teachers why they were so reluctant, and his reply astonished us: The kids weren't used to receiving gifts. They just didn't understand that the backpacks were for them. They thought maybe we just wanted them to look at the backpacks. Once they realized that the backpacks were gifts for them, they were blown away. The other thing that blew them away was the library. They had not been used to having so many books.

While we were there, I noticed one cute little guy with chubby cheeks I couldn't resist. I pinched his cheek, and he didn't like it one bit. "I'm not a girl," he said . . . in English.

Now that blew *me* away. He wanted it to be clear he wasn't a girl, and he didn't like someone pinching his cheek. I should have known better.

One of the most memorable moments of our visit was when one of the young girls stood up in the classroom and made a speech, thanking us for everything we'd done, but especially thanking us for providing books. They were *so* hungry for knowledge and *so* grateful. She told us, "We're going to make you proud."

As I listened to the translation, I cried, tears trickling down my cheeks. I didn't care who saw me.

This eleven-year-old girl talked about how she wanted to become a productive member of society, something that would be achievable thanks to the improved schooling we'd provided. It was the kind of speech you'd be lucky to hear at a school in Middle America. I said to myself, this girl is going to go places. We were so impressed, we arranged for her to travel with us the next day to Macau, where we were holding a major convention. As we prepared to leave the following day, children stood in line in the cold and sang to us as we boarded our bus. For the first time in her life, the girl accompanying us was leaving home, flying on a plane, and traveling out of the country. Then she walked on stage in front of eighteen thousand people to tell them what she'd told us. She was fearless and an inspiration to everyone.

Since then, that girl named Li Meng has certainly made us proud. She is now in high school, and she wants to be more than simply a productive member of society. The encouragement she got from Wendy and me created a mindset shift in her. She now knows that she has great potential, and she wants to be successful.

In 2019, we sponsored a second Chinese community called Gufubao where 30 percent of men and 50 percent of women could not read or write. Winters are cruel, and summers often bring drought. We've already begun to see improvement. More kids attend school and enjoy the breakfast and lunch we provide. Just imagine the difference it makes when a child starts school with a full stomach. At the end of each week, they get a special treat, a dish of chicken legs or dumplings.

The village now has a borehole that services over a hundred acres of agricultural land shared by eighty families, which has boosted harvest yields by 25 percent. Everything interlocks: The water helps grow the crops, which provide the school meals!

Under development in Gufubao are a waste management system and a program to plant two thousand seedling trees to improve soil, provide shade, and grow fresh fruit.

Kenya

Our first venture in Kenya was in 2015 to Irkaat, a village in the Maasai Mara area that's home to 1,800 members of the Kipsigis, Maasai, and Dorobo tribes. The village faced severe drought. The nearest supply of water was more than a mile away and not drinkable. A more reliable source was a silt-filled river an impossible twelve miles distant. There was only one teacher per sixty kids, and they were all doing the best they could in classrooms made of mud or wood.

The villagers often suffered from typhoid, malaria, osteoarthritis, skin diseases, and brucellosis, an infection that's spread from animals to people, usually by unpasteurized dairy products. For children, the most common ailments were diarrhea, kwashiorkor (a severe form of protein deficiency), and upper respiratory tract infections. The nearest place the villagers could get medical attention was six miles distant.

Seventy percent of the villagers live on less than a dollar a day. Most of the men are small-scale subsistence farmers trying to grow beans, maize, and wheat but handicapped by the area's hilly terrain, as well as drought and crop diseases. The women earn money through basket weaving and tailoring.

Thanks to our involvement, a borehole was drilled and a 1,264-gallon tank installed on top of a tower. From this tank, PVC pipe runs underground and connects to the primary school, so all the children in that community now have access to clean drinking water. The borehole water also connects to individual homes, as well as a community water kiosk, so every community member has access to clean water. And the best thing about it is that it's all run by a solar-powered pump to make it efficient and easy to maintain.

Traditionally, the women and girls of the village were responsible for making the mile-long walk to collect water five times a day. Even then, it wasn't clean and caused diseases. Bringing clean water to the village was cause for great celebration. One local woman, Jane Kikwai, led a group of women affectionately known as "mamas" through the village banging empty water containers together as if they were drums. Jane had almost lost her eldest son to typhoid. She knew firsthand what *not* having clean water meant to the health and safety of her children. With the time she saves no longer walking to the river, Jane has opened a small business selling fresh kale, mangoes, avocados, and oranges. With the money from that business, she has bought more land, which her husband farms for maize. The fear that once clung to every sip of water her children took is gone.

Instead of fetching water, girls in the village now attend school. Contributions from Jeunesse Kids have built ten classrooms and a library, and with each classroom we built, the government sent a teacher to the school to ensure lower teacher-to-student ratios. A mobile health clinic visits Irkaat, and health education workshops provide knowledge to reduce preventable diseases. We've also helped educate farmers to improve the nutritional quality of their crops and increase production.

Wendy and I, along with Scott, Craig Kielburger, and about one hundred of our top distributors, witnessed the impact firsthand when we visited in 2016.

After a boneshaking four-hour drive in Land Rovers, we suddenly arrived at this tiny community in the middle of nowhere and were greeted by women and children clapping, dancing, and waving Jeunesse signs. Some of the villagers wore raggedy sports coats—their Sunday best—because it was important to them to show respect. We didn't ask for or need that display, but it was still touching. The girls had shaved their heads, not wanting to waste time fixing their hair first thing in the morning because school started at six or seven and often went until ten at night, six days a week. They have no problem with the long hours because they're so eager to learn, and when the school first opened, the learners never wanted to sleep! But with advice and guidance, the students soon learned that a good night's sleep is important for knowledge retention.

While we were waiting to go into the classroom, these kids invited me to sit in a chair. It was a little plastic chair and looked like it had been around for twenty-five years. I'm not exactly small, and I doubted it could hold my weight, but I didn't want to decline their hospitality and gave it a shot. Sure enough, the chair collapsed, and I lay on the ground with my legs in the air like a cockroach. The kids thought it was hilarious.

A big challenge in Kenya is that there is little opportunity beyond high school. Many children leave the village and even leave the country seeking better prospects elsewhere. "How many of you want to leave Kenya?" I asked.

Every hand went up.

Then I asked, "If you had something you could do here, how many would want to stay?"

Every hand went up again. They didn't want to leave, but they had no choice. There was no way for them to make a living in their home region. If they could work, make money, and support themselves, they wanted to remain. But the deck was stacked against them.

In the meantime, we set up a program for women in the village to make a product that we now sell for them online to our distributors and customers around the world. All the proceeds go to the village. The product is a *rafiki* bracelet made of little beads on string and named for the Swahili word for *friend*. We had a woman go there and show them how to make the bracelets. Wander into the village today and you might see twenty to thirty women sitting under a tree making these bracelets.

One story we heard in Irkaat highlights the challenges of educating young girls in the rural areas of Kenya. Williter Cheshang loved going to school and successfully applied for high school. But her traditionalist father had other ideas. He didn't believe that women needed an education. The day after Williter's application was accepted, her dream of further education was dashed when her father announced he'd arranged for her to be married in exchange for a dowry of goats and blankets. That was her value to him. The headmistress pleaded with him. How could he do such a thing? Williter was a smart girl with a potentially bright future.

Williter's father stuck to his guns until the headmistress came up with a creative offer. She pledged that Williter's value would be much higher once she graduated from high school, and she guaranteed to cover any shortfall if that didn't happen. Williter's father conceded. As it turned out, Williter not only became top of her class but the first girl in the entire state to get an A in English. Her father's tune quickly changed when she was celebrated in the newspapers and people congratulated him. At her graduation ceremony, he sat beaming in the front row wearing a secondhand suit bought for the occasion.

But what next? Shouldn't girls like Williter and those who raised their hand in the classroom have the chance to get a higher education and the possibilities in life that come from that? Craig and Scott decided they all deserved better than a high school education. They needed college, and more than that, they needed to learn how to run a business and generate income. The idea was born to have Jeunesse Kids fund a school for entrepreneurship at the government-accredited WE College. We committed one million dollars to the project, believing that Jeunesse distributors would step in to help, especially those who have overcome hardship in their own lives and succeeded against all the odds. We were sure they would want to pay it forward.

The faculty building has already been designed by an architect, and the strategy behind the School of Entrepreneurship is well underway. Construction on the school is expected to be complete by 2022. We're outfitting it with a student lounge, dormitory, and library. Our funds will enable around twenty-five students annually to learn at the School of Entrepreneurship for years and decades to come. The school will have seasoned and trained lecturers, and a part of the program will involve each student starting a business of their own.

During our visit to Irkaat, the village chief was ecstatic. Kids were going to school. The village had pure water. The farmers had learned better methods to grow more food. As we got ready to leave, he had a large group of children line up to give us high fives to show their appreciation. Last in line was a little boy with snot all over his face. He was barefoot and had holes in his sweater. He looked a wreck. No one wanted to touch him, but I high-fived him, and he latched onto my legs. I walked around with this kid hanging on to me. He wouldn't let me loose, and his snot got all over my legs. It didn't bother me. I felt so connected to him, and my heart went out to him because I knew what it was like to be a kid who is completely ignored.

"We're going to have to leave, but this little guy won't let me go," I said to the teacher.

What the teacher said in reply made me cry.

"He's never had a friend, and he doesn't want to let you go because he doesn't know if he'll find another friend."

If nobody helps kids like this, they're going to be lost to this world.

As we said our good-byes, the chief announced with great ceremony that he had a gift for us. I was more than a little surprised when he presented me with two kid goats. What the hell was I going to do with them? It was a major gift for him to give, and it was a way of recognizing everything we'd done for them, so I couldn't decline the goats. But I also couldn't bring them back to the States. We took them with us, and I later came up with a solution. I regifted the goats to a group of construction workers so they could be put to good use eating the grass and weeds where the guys lived. Well, I hope that's what they did with them, anyway.

On a return visit to Kenya in 2019, a group of Jeunesse volunteers experienced a day in the life of the women—the mamas—in Irkaat. One of their tasks was to walk more than a mile to collect water from a river and then make the trek back with a fifty-pound barrel of water on their backs, something the mamas had done five times a day before we established the clean water supply.

The Jeunesse group was also honored at a ceremony in which tribal elders bestowed Maasai names upon them and handed out gifts of traditional Maasai Shuka, their colorful cloth body wraps.

In 2019, we expanded our support in Kenya to the community of Kesebek in Bomet County, which is made up of 2,200 members of the Kipsigis ethnic group, half of them under the age of eighteen.

Their challenges are similar to those of the Irkaat village. Almost every family relies on subsistence farming, and kids don't get much of an education because they have to work in the fields. Some parents earn a small income laboring on larger farms or selling goats, cows, and sheep.

Our first projects are to get a supply of clean water to them and to provide education about good health practices, more productive farming methods, and financial skills.

Ecuador

Deep in the Amazon jungle, the village of Los Rios in the country of Ecuador has less than three hundred inhabitants. Most students either walk or canoe to their school, which was nothing more than two dilapidated classrooms with sagging roofs and dirt floors before we came to help. The village's water supply was a health hazard, leading to diseases like cholera, which killed a disproportionate number of children, as well as gastrointestinal illnesses, malnutrition, high mercury levels in the blood, and mosquito-borne and zoonotic (animal to human) diseases. The villagers had the worst health in the country.

Through our contributions, the school has new classrooms, along with a kitchen and dining hall and a school garden. Not surprisingly, more kids are going to school. Jeunesse Kids also stepped in financially and physically, helping to construct a water tank to deliver clean water to the school and all of the homes.

On the health front, apart from the benefits of clean water, we've provided mobile clinics and workshops on preventive care. Women in the village also now earn income making the same kind of *rafiki* bracelets as the villagers in Kenya.

Led by Craig Kielburger, a team of volunteers including Jeunesse employees, distributors, and their families, visited the village on a Bringing Hope trip in 2017.

The Jeunesse team had the opportunity to attend a diploma ceremony at the school and inspect the Jeunesse-funded garden in which children grow healthy fruits and vegetables. Jeunesse Kids also created a group for girls and young women that provides craft skills, as well as financial and leadership training.

Perhaps the most heartwarming moment of the trip was hearing ninety-nine-year-old grandmother, Rosa Granja, say, "I never thought I'd see clean water in my lifetime."

India

The remote village of Kalinjar in the northwestern part of India has a population of under nine hundred. Malnutrition is a key health concern. Most villagers are poor and illiterate. They survive by working as unskilled day laborers for two dollars a day or by growing maize on small plots of land, severely hampered by an erratic water supply. The village well only provided water for three months of the year. The source for the remaining months was a muddy creek.

At the school, the conditions for learning were appalling. Children grades one through ten had to sit hunched on the floor in small, dark, poorly ventilated rooms with walls and floors covered in fungus and mildew from years of water seepage during the monsoon season.

All the students and teachers shared one cramped, unventilated latrine that had no running water or septic system. Their source of water was community hand pumps or open wells, often contaminated with pollutants such as fecal matter. Sadly, community members lacked basic knowledge of sanitary and hygiene practices.

We quickly built two new schoolrooms and furnished them so the kids don't have to squat on the floor. A CNN segment that highlighted how education is transforming villages in India described it as a big boon to the community.

We are improving the water supply with wells and water tanks feeding into water fountains, and we built school latrines and a septic system. We gave villagers health training covering basic hygiene and illness-prevention practices and emphasizing the importance of clean water and sanitation, things that we take for granted in the Western world.

But we didn't stop there. We began livelihood and income opportunity programs, which included women's empowerment and business training. Our team showed them how to improve farming practices to increase crop yields and raise farm animals. They had little scrub goats worth nothing and cows that were just skin and bones. We replaced the goats with twenty Sirohi goats, which can have three kids a year and give lots of milk. We replaced the cows with cows that were more productive in producing butterfat.

Our Bringing Hope visit was the first time a group of foreigners was welcomed to the community, and we were treated with much honor and ceremony. It was heartwarming to see the kids sitting at their desks with pencils and notebooks in their hands for the first time in their lives. It was a Sunday, and not all of the teachers were there, so some of our group stepped in to give them lessons.

A Bringing Hope trip also gives our distributors the chance to experience other aspects of a country. In this case that meant visits to several places: the majestic Taj Mahal; Jaipur, the capital of the state of Rajasthan, known as the pink city because of the color of many of its buildings; and the national capital, New Delhi, a place with a seething mass of humanity frantically going about its daily business.

In 2020, we began to help a second village in India, Antri. Sixty-five percent of the villagers there are subsistence farmers in tribal and lower caste populations. Under conditions that include unreliable rainfall, they grow maize on small fragmented plots of land. It's almost impossible for them to produce enough food for their families. The community lacks access to basic services such as education, water, and health care.

Through our assistance, a derelict school building is being replaced with three modern structures and schoolrooms. The school latrines are being renovated, and clean water is being provided. As with other villages, we've provided education on basic hygiene and illness prevention, agricultural training, financial literacy training, and women's empowerment and business training.

Most of the villagers' homes were constantly filled with lung-damaging smoke from the use of chullahs, their traditional clay stove. The solution we provided: *smokeless* chullahs.

Local Initiatives

Village sponsorships in the Third World is not the only way Jeunesse makes a difference. When Jeunesse Global holds major events in cities across the globe, we have a Jeunesse Kids fundraising campaign to support good causes locally. These charitable initiatives are primarily for children and focus on projects that yield long-term benefits such as renovating and building schools and homes, providing lifesaving medical equipment, and offering education.

Since 2012, we've raised more than eleven million dollars, five million of which have been raised in the last two years alone. In 2018, we collected $1.57 million in five cities with conventions attended by 62,500 people. One remarkable event in Macau raised a staggering $1.13 million. In our hometown of Orlando, we had donations of more than $220,000 for Kids Beating Cancer to match children with potentially life-saving bone marrow or stem cell donors.

We raised funds around the world for important causes: in Rio de Janeiro, $133,000 for the Association for Assistance of Disabled Children (AACD) Children's Rehabilitation Hospital to aid disabled children live a full life; in Los Angeles, $128,831 for Ronald McDonald House for renovations to the pediatrics wing; in Bangkok, $45,862 for Community Children Foundation for clean water, food security, and simple family income initiatives in which children can participate (such as raising egg-bearing chickens.)

Our wonderful distributors raised more than $40,000 in each of three other locations: Berlin, to help Charité Hospital Berlin renovate its adolescent eating disorders clinic; Kuala Lumpur, for infrastructure and clean water projects at Majilis Belia Orang Asli (MBOA) Children's Orphanage; Rome, for the Andrea Bocelli Foundation to help rebuild a school destroyed in the central Italy earthquakes.

In 2019, the Jeunesse EXPO World Tour featured stops in five cities—Orlando, Singapore, Bangkok, Milan, and Rio de Janeiro—attracting fifty thousand attendees who raised $1.5 million.

Jeunesse Kids collected a record-breaking $395,000 at the first stop in Orlando for our local charity initiative Kids Beating Cancer. But we weren't done. Scott surprised the audience by announcing that we were topping up the distributor donations to fully fund the one million dollars the charity needed for their state-of-the-art cancer cellular therapy lab.

Distributor Contributions

When we launched Jeunesse Kids, we told our distributors that we were fortunate enough to have more money than we needed and that we wanted to give back and help others. We set an example and said that we hoped those who became successful would also give back and help others. And that's what they do.

In our company incentives program, when distributors achieve Triple Diamond Director rank, they get a one-time cash bonus of one hundred thousand dollars. Four distributors who have reached this level have donated their bonus to Jeunesse Kids and are recognized as Distinguished Jeunesse Kids Champions.

In addition, some leaders have supported their own charitable endeavors. Triple Diamond Directors Tom and Theresa Gregory have built a school in Uganda and supported many orphanages. "Not only have we been able to help out with Jeunesse Kids, which is the heartbeat of Jeunesse, but we have also been able to expand our own business and ministry around the world."

Diamond Directors Paula Pritchard and Kathy Robbins came to Jeunesse after "a boatload of bad experiences" with other network marketing companies. Their success has enabled them to be substantial donors to an elephant sanctuary, the Humane Society, and an animal rescue called Red Rover that saves animals after natural disasters.

When major tragedies strike, we always want to do our part. When Australia was ravaged by bushfires in its 2019–2020 season, killing thirty-four people and one billion animals and destroying 2,800 homes, Jeunesse Kids stepped in with a donation of one hundred thousand dollars, primarily to help children traumatized or displaced by the life-altering event.

And then, when the world was ravaged by the COVID-19 pandemic, we contributed five hundred thousand dollars to the World Health Organization's COVID-19 Solidarity Response Fund. The donation goes toward funding the activities of WHO's Strategic Preparedness and Response Plan, which includes tracking and understanding the virus, ensuring patients get care, acquiring protective gear for front-line workers, and accelerating efforts to develop vaccines, tests, and treatments.

When you see the results of what we've been able to achieve through Jeunesse Kids, and especially for kids in villages, it's wonderful. They're so happy and appreciative to have been given something. It's heartwarming to look into the eyes of these children and see unconditional love.

I'm grateful to have found joy and to have given joy. And there's a lot more joy we can give and get. Jeunesse Kids is the vehicle for Wendy and me to get there.

Chapter 10

Looking Ahead

"Live a life that matters. Live a life of love."

Where do we go from here? Upward, of course. While we were thrilled to be recognized on the *Direct Selling News* Global 100 list as the thirteenth biggest-selling direct sales company in the world, the message to us was that there were twelve companies ahead of Jeunesse.

We've hit as high as $1.46 billion in annual sales, but household-name network marketing companies that have been in business a heck of a lot longer report four billion dollars, five billion dollars, and Amway, the granddaddy of them all, over eight billion in annual sales.

So that has to be our goal: to become number one, and as much as we respect its culture and longtime success, to knock Amway off its pedestal. We still have some catching up to do, especially in the domestic market.

We're probably the best-kept billion-dollar secret in America even though we've already helped hundreds of thousands of people achieve their goals and dreams. With the quality of our dedicated team, the uniqueness of our products, and our innovation, we're creating a legacy. We just have to stay disciplined and consistent, hungry and humble. We can't stop now. We feel like we have to do it forever. The bigger and stronger we become in country after country, the more children we can help.

Wendy and I are at a time in our lives when it would be easy to say we deserve to take it easy. We've worked damn hard all our lives and achieved enormous success, so why not rest on our laurels, sit by the swimming pool, soak up the Florida sunshine, and reflect on everything we've accomplished? Instead, we're driven to build a legacy company in the network marketing industry that will continue long after we're gone.

So far, we've established a solid footprint around the world, and we'll keep expanding. We'll continue to develop innovative products and marketing strategies, surrounded by an award-winning team that excels in every aspect of the business and is capable of overcoming any challenge that is thrown in our path. Because that's what we do.

While I was writing this book, the COVID-19 pandemic struck from nowhere, a once-in-a-century crisis that has impacted every family in one way or another.

How did we react?

The first thing we did was make that half a million dollar donation through Jeunesse Kids to the World Health Organization COVID-19 Solidarity Response Fund, which is administered in partnership with the United Nations Foundation and Swiss Philanthropy Foundation.

Second, in response to the acute shortage of hand sanitizers, we rushed into production our own AlōClnz™ Hand Sanitizer, an ethyl alcohol product boosted with aloe vera.

Third, we stepped up our ability to communicate online. Our Jeunesse Live, broadcast worldwide on a platform that can hold thirty thousand people at a time listening to live translations in eight languages, is a more effective way than ever to communicate personally and directly with distributors everywhere. It is a dynamic way to inspire and inform in troubled times. We have a rock-solid team that was well prepared ahead of time to seamlessly switch into a virtual work-from-home operation. If we don't have great employees, we don't have a business, so we moved heaven and earth to enable everyone but warehouse staff to work remotely. The whole has to be greater than the sum of its parts.

From charitable giving, to product development, to expanded communication, Jeunesse immediately began the process of operating in this new environment.

We're thankful that the network marketing industry, and Jeunesse in particular, provides financial hope not only during a crisis like COVID-19 but also after the crisis ends, especially for those who find there is no job to go back to. It is at times like these that the benefits of a work from home business become most apparent. Given the right tools, plenty of people can turn their lives around, and that's what I like most about this business.

Think about it. Because the company has invested in state-of-the-art technological infrastructure, distributors can contact prospective customers and distributors anywhere in the world. In turn, they order products direct from the company, which drop-ships those products to their front door. There is no need to meet face-to-face. From anywhere, using their laptop or their smartphone, distributors can build a business to supplement their income or replace lost income.

Historically, network marketing is the industry that has not just survived but thrived during economic downturns and recessions. When income options are limited, smart and resourceful people seek viable alternatives and often find their way to a business that has a low start-up cost, low overhead, and low risk. People who thought they had a golden career path or a guaranteed full-time job and those who previously expressed disinterest in network marketing sometimes have a change of mind during times of depression and recession. Remember too that network marketing is a business in which spouses can work together as they strive to rebuild after suffering a financial calamity. In times of adversity, entrepreneurial spirit flares.

The COVID-19 epidemic may well have changed the way the world does business in the future. Traditional companies may find that they don't need downtown high-rises (or at least not so many), having discovered that employees could easily operate from a home base.

It's something we've known for years. We've also known that network marketing can be a fun, exciting business. If you're passionate and work hard, you can be successful—very successful. It's the perfect way to help others and give back. I feel that if you conceive of it and believe in it, you can achieve it.

We've personally enjoyed success, and while the fact that Jeunesse is a billion-dollar company is one way of measuring that success, it's not the best way. It's more rewarding for us to know that there are thousands of other people who have accomplished more than they ever dreamed possible because we've partnered together to share Jeunesse products and the Jeunesse opportunity.

My dad was the wisest man I ever met. Another of his famous expressions was this: "We all leave this world with empty pockets." He was an uneducated man but a wise man. He knew what he was talking about. It's what we do during our lives to help others that counts.

Someone else who knew what he or she was talking about was the person who wrote the anonymous lines below that have circulated on the internet. They perfectly express the way that Wendy and I feel about life's journey, and they represent an ideal way to bring my story to a close:

At the end of life, what really matters
is not what we bought, but what we built;
not what we got, but what we shared;
not our competence, but our character;
and not our success, but our significance.
Live a life that matters. Live a life of love.

Acknowledgments

I've lived a wonderful life that has been enriched by so many people across many countries, but I would be remiss if I did not acknowledge some special individuals.

First, foremost, and forever is Wendy, my partner in everything. My life would not be complete without her and even after all of these years she still laughs (sometimes) at my jokes.

I have to thank my two brothers.

My older brother James Reginald (JR) Ray made a major contribution to my life by giving up his teenage years to work and make sure our family had food to eat. He also became my guardian angel who kept me from getting into too much trouble.

My younger brother Winfred Alton (Turkey) Ray was my primary friend, because I had no other. He was the best mud pie maker. At times, we were so hungry he'd pat mud from the creek bank into a hamburger-like patty, and that would be our dinner.

My sister Wanda Jean Ray was special, and not just because she was my only sister.

After all these years, Betty Mills is still one of my best friends. She and her husband Jerry got married on my birthday one year, and I make a point of visiting them whenever I'm in the area. Betty's mom gave me a pair of her Easter shoes to wear when I was nine years old. I got teased for that, but I was glad to have the shoes so I wouldn't have to go barefoot.

Gerald Mills and his wife Gail: a very sweet couple. Gerald would buy me a Dreamsicle every time the ice cream truck came by. Gail was the daughter of my favorite teacher in fourth grade and a star on the girls' basketball team. Her dad was our mail carrier.

What can I say about my Jeunesse Family? We've grown to be a family of 675,000 spread across more than 145 countries. Wendy and I have shared precious moments with many of you as we've worked together to make Jeunesse the company that it is today. I appreciate every one of you and especially those who have not only contributed to the growth of the business but also our nonprofit foundation Jeunesse Kids.

The Jeunesse Global corporate team has also grown, and is now almost a thousand strong. I'm impressed every day by your commitment and enthusiasm. Jennifer Luce, our vice president of global human resources, has been a valuable presence at my side for many years, and she has grown with the company.

Finally, I've wanted to write this book for a long time, and it would not have come to fruition without the assistance of Malcolm Nicholl. Even though he's British, he sculpted exactly what this boy from Tennessee wanted to say and how he wanted to say it. Thank you guv'nor.

About the Author

Randy Ray is an award-winning entrepreneur and philanthropist. Three businesses that he cofounded with wife Wendy Lewis have appeared on the *Inc. 500* list of Fastest-Growing Private Companies in America.

Under Randy's leadership, Jeunesse Global was the youngest company in direct selling history to reach billion-dollar annual sales and has ranked as high as number thirteen in the world on the *Direct Selling News* Global 100 list.

Randy has been honored more than twenty times in several prestigious business awards programs for Lifetime Achievement, Executive of the Year, Founding Team of the Year, and Management Team of the Year.

With a giant-size heart for giving back, his greatest pleasure is the success of the Jeunesse Kids nonprofit foundation that he and Wendy established to give impoverished children across the world a brighter future.

Randy divides his time between his homes in Florida, California, North Carolina, and seat 6A on long-haul flights.

Jeunesse Kids Champions Honor Roll

We consider everyone who contributes to Jeunesse Kids a Champion. That's why we were inspired to establish the Jeunesse Kids Champions program, which recognizes those who have shown outstanding servant leadership with their contributions to our nonprofit organization. The Jeunesse Kids Champions program acknowledges cumulative donations at different levels.

I am so humbled by the leaders who live with purpose, live with passion, and live Jeunesse: the leaders who make it to the top and then make it their top priority to give back. We had the honor of recognizing these generous leaders as Jeunesse Kids Champions at the EXPO Next event in Orlando, Florida, in September 2019.

Elite Jeunesse Kids Champions
Gifts of $250,000 to $499,999

Kim Hui	Presidential Diamond Director
Jennifer Chen	Triple Diamond Director

Distinguished Jeunesse Kids Champions
Gifts of $100,000 to $249,999

Tom & Theresa Gregory	Triple Diamond Directors
Ming Lee	Double Diamond Director
Flora Li	Triple Diamond Director

Honored Jeunesse Kids Champions
Gifts of $25,000 to $99,999

Sannie Nie	Double Diamond Director
Paula Pritchard & Kathy Robbins	Diamond Directors
Min Xu Ruckle	Double Diamond Director
Michelle Song	Double Diamond Director
Helen Zhang	Double Diamond Director

Through every donation to Jeunesse Kids, we're building brighter tomorrows for young people. We're so thankful for the support of our Jeunesse Family, including these incredible Jeunesse Kids Champions.

We honor those who live by this principle: You make a living by what you get, but you make a life by what you give.

Learn more about Jeunesse Kids at: *https://www.jeunessekids.org*

Jeunesse Kids makes historic $1 million donation to Kids Beating
Cancer at the Jeunesse EXPO NEXT 2019 in Orlando.

Together We Are Making a Difference

I have a special place in my heart for kids born into dire
circumstances. That's why all proceeds from the sale of this book
support Jeunesse Kids, our 501(c)(3) nonprofit foundation.
Thank you for helping me bring its mission to life.

Randy Ray